H. B. JACOBINI

UNIVERSITY OF ALABAMA

A STUDY OF THE PHILOSOPHY
OF INTERNATIONAL LAW
AS SEEN IN WORKS OF
LATIN AMERICAN WRITERS

MARTINUS NIJHOFF / THE HAGUE

A STUDY OF THE PHILOSOPHY OF
INTERNATIONAL LAW AS SEEN IN WORKS
OF LATIN AMERICAN WRITERS

H. B. JACOBINI

UNIVERSITY OF ALABAMA

A STUDY OF THE PHILOSOPHY
OF INTERNATIONAL LAW
AS SEEN IN WORKS OF
LATIN AMERICAN WRITERS

MARTINUS NIJHOFF / THE HAGUE / 1954

PRINTED IN THE NETHERLANDS

TO MY WIFE

ACKNOWLEDGEMENTS

The writer wishes to acknowledge the assistance which he has received from many quarters throughout the entire period of research, translation, and writing. A special word of gratitude is tendered to Professor W. E. SANDELIUS of the University of Kansas whose careful and kindly criticisms and suggestions have been of great value, and to the writer's wife for her assistance in proofreading and in numerous other ways in the preparation of the text.

TABLE OF CONTENTS

INTRODUCTION

One of the most unfortunate facts about the relationship of the United States with Latin America is that only in recent years has there been any appreciable amount of intellectual interchange with reference to law. This, of course, is an example of the relative lack of cultural exchange between these peoples. Only in very recent years has the North American interest in Latin America been in any sense general and active.

While there are a few recent volumes which discuss various aspects of Latin American law in a fashion calculated to interest the North American lawyer and academician, the Latin American contributions to and attitudes toward *international* law are virtually unknown in the United States except in very restricted quarters.

For this reason it was thought that a survey such as the one presented here would contribute not only to a better understanding of Latin American juristic thought as pertaining to international law, but also to a better comprehension of legal theory in general, and of Latin American culture as a whole.

The phase of the philosophy of international law which, with reference to the regional application here studied, has been the major interest in this work, *i.e.*, whether writers rely more on naturalism or positivism as the philosophical foundation of the law of nations, is, like the matter of Latin American law itself, a subject which has been neglected by North American scholars. Most textbook and treatise writers, in the field of international law, however, have at least something to say about legal philosophy, if nothing more than to survey the predominant orientations of a few of the more important writers from the middle of the fifteenth century to quite recent times. The philosophical content of most general studies of international law is a hazy intimation that positivism represents modern enlightenment as contrasted with the superstition of an earlier day, but little

1

effort is taken to establish any legal theory by means other than simple suggestion, and for this reason too it was thought that the present survey might be able to make some contribution to a needed clarification.

It may not be amiss to mention at this point that the present writer's interest in this general topic stemmed from a realization that a shortcoming in his experience as a teacher was a feeling of inadequacy when attempting to discuss the foundations of international law.

As has already been mentioned, treatise writers are often sufficiently interested in the matter of the foundations of international law to briefly mention it, but more often than not the remarks regarding the problem are not particularly illuminating or informative except in an historical sense. One of the reasons for this tendency to avoid the depths of this issue may well be the very real fact that positivists and naturalists are found on both sides of virtually every important practical question, and that there is little indication that either avowed orientation would consistently represent a more enlightened view than the other. Von Treitschke and Austin, for example, held similar views on sovereignty but each represented a different philosophical orientation; similarly, Kelsen and Le Fur, though both monists, represent positivism and naturalism respectively; and, in an interrogative vein, could there be, any appreciable difference among the views of positivists, eclectics, and naturalists as to a principle such, for example, as that of the *thalweg*?

What, then, is the significance of this whole question? In a certain sense as, for example, in the instances mentioned above, the matter may have very little significance. On the other hand, the problem of whether justice requires natural law with which positive law can be compared and improved is of a fundamental sort, and it remains a persistent issue in that while interest in it may wane for a time it seems always to be revived at a later moment. Currently there is considerable attention being shown to the matter.

To point up this fact clearly but succinctly there would seem to be no better way than to note the pronouncements of two noted scholars in the field on international law who, while both are considered to be inclined toward a progressive point of view, represent markedly different philosophical orientations. It has been said "... that all philosophy of law of this generation will necessarily have to be a 'dialogue with Kelsen' " [1]. Whether or not this is a sound judgement need not be debated here since for purposes of this discussion it may be noted simply that Hans Kelsen's statement is as emphatic a presentation of legal positivism as the present writer has seen, and perhaps the clearest ever written. The naturalistic orientation of Hersh Lauterpacht, on the other hand, is a well thought through position which reveals, in its contrast with Kelsen's view, the philosophical importance and nature of this entire problem.

The founder of the Vienna school, Hans Kelsen, in a recent sketch of the history of the natural law view, found to his own satisfaction that natural law has been used to support both sides of the more important social and intellectual issues as reflected in law, and, therefore, that its validity as a body of norms to govern social conduct is at best of questionable merit. The use of natural law both to defend and to attack monarchy, as by Filmer and Locke, or socialism, as by Comte and Spencer, is cited among others as examples of the alleged duplicity of natural law. Agreeing with Plato that a lie may at times be useful in supporting the ends of government [2], Kelsen makes it quite clear that he considers natural law to be only a lie which nevertheless may be thought by some to be useful [3].

There is evidence presented elsewhere that Kelsen does not deny the value of metaphysical considerations, but his view is that the objects of these on the one hand and matters of a temporal character on the other are to be surveyed with absolutely no reference to each other [4]. Seemingly it is on this premise that Kelsen's attack on natural law is based.

In the last analysis, however, as far as the question of the nature of justice is concerned, there is nothing which could be more emphatic than Kelsen's statement of positivism, and he leaves absolutely no doubt that he considers natural law to be unadulterated nonsense.

[1] Josef L. Kunz, *Latin-American Philosophy of Law in the Twentieth Century* (New York, Inter-American Law Institute, 1950), p. 74.
[2] Hans Kelsen, 'The Natural-Law Doctrine Before the Tribunal of Science' *The Western Political Quarterly* Vol II, pp. 481–513.
[3] *Ibid.*, p. 513.
[4] Kunz, *loc. cit.*

The English international lawyer, Hersh Lauterpacht, on the other hand, who seems of late to be primarily interested in the legal personality of the individual under international law, is quite emphatic that this status of the individual man, and indeed personal rights of many sorts, are the result of a realization of the natural right of the individual as such to a degree of respect [5].

Lauterpacht is well aware that natural law has been used to support both sides of many questions, but strongly affirms that its chief application has been to the "... defence of the imprescriptible rights of the liberty and the equality of man" [6]. This function of natural law, he says, is the "... continuous thread in the historical pattern of legal and political thought" [7].

The natural law, in Lauterpacht's view, is not a series of absolute norms, clear and concise on every point at all times in human experience. Rather,

It moulds the minds of rulers and legislators by instilling into them that degree of reasonableness and restraint which constitutes the barrier between obedience and rebellion [8].

One apprehends it, therefore, through a sort of intuition of the just, as something like the realization of a consensus of justice in the Krabbean view. But it must not be thought of as being solely a product of ratiocination; according to Lauterpacht, a realization of the precepts of natural law results from experience [9].

The point of this perusal of a few of the ideas of two of the Western World's leading international legists on the matter of naturalism vs. positivism is to suggest in some small measure the importance which juristic thinkers are disposed to impute to this issue regarding the basis of law.

It should be mentioned here in passing that the terms natural law and positive law each suggests more than one type of legal or philosophical arrangement. Without in any way attempting to exhaust the point, it may be observed that natural law on

---

[5] H. Lauterpacht, *International Law and Human Rights* (New York, Frederick A. Praeger, Inc., 1950), pp. 73–126.
[6] *Ibid.*, p. iii.
[7] *Ibid.*, p. 80.
[8] Ibid., p. 93.
[9] Ibid., pp. 97–100.

the one hand may suggest a sort of divinely ordered scheme of things such as was envisioned by the Stoics and the clerical doctors of the middle ages; it may suggest a legal system in which only precepts of natural law are legally valid, as held by Pufendorf; it may imply the idea of natural rights of man in the sense of eighteenth century rationalism; or it may postulate an intuition of the just as a guide to legislation much as suggested by Lauterpacht. Positivism, on the other hand, usually refers to the notion of law as enacted or otherwise formulated by man himself. The Austinian system, which recognized as law only those rules sanctioned by the sovereign, is perhaps the classic example of positivism, but other examples would include the reliance upon enacted treaties and established customs of international law as emphasized by such authorities as William E. Hall and August W. Heffter, also the reformist schemes of the self-styled positivists, Leon Duguit and Hans Kelsen.

As a rule of thumb it may be suggested that conceptions which conceive of any law, juridical or moral, as superior to the enacted law are to be termed natural law conceptions, while systems which recognize only enacted law, whether by monistic sovereignity or by pluralistic agreement, or crystalized custom, are positivist in character. It is important to realize, however, that a great many writers and thinkers recognize the value of both positivist and naturalist elements in legal thought, and attempt to utilize them together in eclectic combinations of various sorts. This eclecticism is perhaps more characteristic of jurists interested in international law than of legists concerned with municipal law because international law is not as closely tied to particular legislative forms as is national law, and jurists of the latter interest can more easily than their internationalist colleagues center their attention on the mere form and the immediate source of law.

In the domestic area, then, it is not too difficult to think of law *per se* as mere form and, consequently, to leave to legislative bodies, for the most part, the function of setting up the just norms. This is due, it would seem, to the relatively high degree of stability which obtains in the domestic order. This stability is not in itself the essence of a legal system; rather, it is the attribute of a social situation which allows of a particular type of juridical arrangement — generally one which tends to glorify tradition and to disparage change.

It is true, of course, that in times of crisis law in the domestic sphere frequently tends toward rapid adjustment, while precedents, at these times, become of less relative weight. Examples of this can be seen in the legislation of the Great Depression and in the subsequent court decisions in the United States during the nineteen-thirties. This tendency can be seen to an extent in the cases involving the Japanese-American displaced persons during the period of World War II. It appears in the extremist movements in Italy, Germany, and Russia in the present century, and in the social revolution of contemporary England. Relatively, however, as compared with international relationships, the domestic sphere has exemplified stability.

While relative stability has often obtained also in the international sphere, its prevalence has tended to be less general there than in the domestic realm, and it is not merely coincidental that the theorists of legal positivism have been, in general, more widely received by those interested in municipal law than by those of a more internationalist orientation.

It is not suggested, of course, that positivism has left international law unscathed, and that the latter's allegiance to natural law, or to the concept of justice as distinguished from, and as sometimes over-riding, the positive law, has been a constant. Manifestly no such view has been taken in this work, but it is significant that the writers of international law have, on the whole, been less Austinian than the Austinians, *i.e.*, less rigidly positivist than the domestic legists. Positivism in international law has been either of a less rigid or of a more revolutionary sort than its domestic counterpart. It has looked in times past as well as present primarily toward treaties and customs, but has often recognized also the power of the idea of justice as a real force in the juridical process. Especially in quite recent times it has taken forms which, while in themselves of a radical but positivist character, retain often (as in the case of Duguit) implied overtones of innate justice and equity. Even the positivist view of Kelsen, while rigidly characterized as such, in placing international above domestic law in the hierarchy of norms, appeals to the internationalist's own sense of justice; for it is being directed at an apparent evil in the world order, namely national sovereignty, and indeed, a naturalist might well ask whether this practical recognition of the just by avowed positivists is not to be attributed to their innate, though to be sure unrecognized, intuition of justice.

It is submitted, then, that instability and need for change have made students of international law less skittish about the recognition of natural law (whether called thus or by some other term such as equity, justice or international decency) as an element in the law, than has been true of writers interested fundamentally in domestic law; and in Latin America, with which the body of this work is primarily concerned, the natural law element, whether of Thomist or Kantian origin, has appeared with remarkable consistency in the writings on international law from the earliest works on the matter to the present.

Although the Latin Americans, for the most part, have followed the general trends of the Western World in matters of international law, there were virtually none in that continent who disregarded natural law entirely, and it is significant that all of the writers surveyed in the body of this work have been eclectics at least to a degree.

On the other hand, the most influential of these writers would seem to be those who have emphasized the positive aspects of international law and who have relegated the naturalistic features to a secondary role.

It is evident from what has just been said that the problem of determining whether the Latin American writers are positivists or naturalists is not one of absolutely separating the sheep from the goats, but rather a relative problem in which a greater or lesser degree of each of these elements is determined.

The question of the international personality of the individual, while not of necessity closely connected with that of naturalism vs. positivism, is, nevertheless, a modern theoretical problem of international law which is of the highest significance, and one with which the following survey will definitely concern itself. This matter, because of the question of allegiance and of the feeling of an actual and intimate relationship, is closely tied up with the problems of the breakdown of national sovereignty, the curbing of the irresponsible predatory state, the development of international authority, and the growth of a sentiment of community consciousness in the international realm. That the development of the individual as a subject of international law, as well as a realization of the other goals just mentioned, can be achieved on either naturalistic or positivistic premises is manifest from a study of these positions. However, with reference to the indication of some trend toward recognition of the international personality of the individual, this represents a highly significant change from what, until recently, was considered a fundamental axiom of the law of nations. It may be suggested that this new development involves a feeling or belief that the new point of view will achieve justice more readily than will the *status quo*, and in this sense the issue is quite closely related to the general idea of natural law. It must be emphasized, however, that the naturalism involved is often of a broadly philosophical and political nature rather than of a strictly juristic character.

Although, as has just been pointed out, there is good ground for relating this matter to natural law, the consideration here of the problem of the international personality of the individual as having a part in the present survey of Latin American philosophy of international law has not been conceived of as being intimately bound up with the issue of positivism vs. naturalism. Rather, it has been considered as the foremost theoretical problem confronting modern international law and, consequently, as sufficiently important to merit some treatment in a work purporting to inquire as to the underlying legal philosophy of writers on international law.

It is largely but not exclusively with this in mind that advocates of the "new international law" have been treated here. These writers, whether in Europe or America, have usually emphasized the twin elements which are the international personality of the individual and the diminution of national sovereignty as a counterpart of an augmented international community. Several of these last mentioned works have been considered also from the standpoint of their over-all philosophical and practical systems in an attempt to present some of the more important "seeker" elements in Latin America as they pertain to international law. These works, often of a hybrid character, show influences of diverse origin among which may be mentioned a sociological orientation smacking strongly of Krabbe and especially of Duguit, of natural law in a relatively modern sense, and, to a limited degree, the pure theory of law. There are also a number of systems which, with relatively little interest in the theoretical aspects, attempt in quite an original fashion to set forth practical plans for the rejuvenation of the law of nations.

The third element included in this work is a survey of the so-called American school of international law. It was felt that a résumé of the philosophy of international law as seen in the works of Latin American writers could not avoid some treatment of this particularist theory unless it should restrict itself entirely to the problem of naturalism vs. positivism. Since, as has been suggested above, such a restriction was not thought to be entirely applicable here, the inclusion of a survey of this regional concept would seem to be required.

It may further be stated that the *American* school of international law is really quite closely related to some of the elements in the new international law, and it might even have been considered as part of the latter somewhat heterogeneous tradition.

All of this material is presented against the background of a survey of the theory of international law in the Western World since the fifteenth century.

A few words need to be said with reference to the choice of sources, and to the research techniques and methods of presentation employed.

A. *As to Sources*

1. Most of the works consulted have been systematic treatises and class textbooks. Reliance on these works was based on the hypothesis that the more important views would find expression there, and that these works would show a truer cross section of Latin American thought on these matters than would any other collection of sources. All of the nineteenth century works which could be located were included, this scope being a practical possibility in view of the number published. The twentieth century works were selected largely with a view to

choosing the most widely known and highly respected representative authorities, but with some attempt also to achieve
wide geographical distribution. It was felt that the degree of
completeness attained for the nineteenth century was not a
practical possibility for the present century in view of the vastly
greater amount of literature available. The method of selection,
it must be emphasized, is thought to be quite representative.

2. The works of Juan Bautista Alberdi and also those having
to do largely with the new international law were chosen perhaps
less systematically. Alberdi was included largely because his
modern thinking seemed logically to precede the new international law and because of his stature among Latin American
thinkers.

The works of the new international law were chosen with a
view to representing the more important elements of this tradition.

3. Three types of studies were selected in order to assay the
American school of international law. These were (a) those works
which supported the thesis that a characteristically American
international law exists, (b) those works which could be expected
to be antagonistic to this view, and (c) a number of systematic
treatises largely by writers who were not known to have participated actively in the polemic, and whose opinions were recorded
in an effort to get a cross section of enlightened Latin American
opinion on the issue.

B. As to Techniques of Research and Presentation

1. The works represented in item 1 under A above were dealt
with in the following fashion: the chapters in each of these
works which were concerned with the nature, sources, and
foundations of international law were carefully surveyed in an
effort to determine each writer's philosophical orientation. Where
no such chapter or section existed, other pertinent parts of the
work were studied.

2. In an effort to determine each writer's attitude toward
the idea of the individual as a subject of international law, the
definition of each was carefully analyzed, and, where available,
the sections on the subjects or persons of international law
were studied.

3. In recognition of the strength of the reform movement in Latin America as well as throughout the world in general, a number of works were selected as outstanding examples of important and representative views, and an attempt was made to survey a number of these in detail and to summarize a few others.

4. In Chapters II and III each writer's work has been presented individually. In general, they have been grouped chronologically (with reference to publication date) within the classifications into which they have been placed, but the writers of the new international law were surveyed in a sequence calculated to place related viewpoints in as close proximity to each other as possible rather than with reference to chronology. No attempt has been made to group writers according to nationality as it early became apparent that such a classification would have little juristic significance. The only exception to this rule was the mention of the works of Americano and Marinho which together were labeled as a unique Brazilian tradition.

5. In each case enough evidence has been presented to give the reader a clear view of the considerations which determined the classification. An attempt has been made, however, to refrain from citing more evidence than is absolutely necessary.

6. The principal writings on both sides of the controversy over American international law were outlined. An analysis was made of the entire problem in terms of the actual extent of these particularist norms and of competent Latin American juridical opinion regarding the matter.

It should be added that every effort has been made throughout to select works of an influential and representative character to the end of presenting as true and as comprehensive a picture as possible of the theory of international law in Latin America.

CHAPTER I

GENERAL PHILOSOPHICAL BACKGROUND

A. THE 15TH, 16TH, 17TH AND 18TH CENTURIES

When speaking of the schools of international law it is customary to refer to three [1]: the positivist, the naturalist, and the eclectic or Grotian. These schools shade into one another, however, and each term is applied to several different conceptions of international law. Furthermore, the relationships among these various views of the law of nations, historically speaking, are often quite intricate.

Among the precursors of HUGO GROTIUS [2] (1583–1645) the representatives of two divergent points of view must be noted, both of which were utilized by the "father of international law". The philosophical system which he followed was in some measure suggested by the writings of the Spanish clerics, both professors, FRANCISCO VITORIA [3] (1480–1546) and FRANCISCO SUÁREZ (1548–1617). These two men, whose orientation was theological rather than juridical, recognized the fact that internationalism was coming to replace the medieval concept of universality, but they clung to the scholastic method and argued in Thomistic terms. Both, for example, emphasized the view that the natural law was basic, but that a secondary positive law was not to be denied [4]. "The human race", observed Suárez,

---

[1] L. Oppenheim, *International Law A Treatise* (London, Longmans, Green and Company, 1948), pp. 91–94. Also, Charles G. Fenwick, *International Law* (New York, Appleton-Century-Crofts, Inc., 1948), pp. 53–57. Also, Llewellyn Pfankuchen, *A Documentary Textbook in International Law* (New York, Farrar and Rinehart, Inc., 1940), p. 7.

[2] Hugo Grotius, *De jure belli ac pacis libri tres*, 1645 edition, 2 vols. (*The Classics of International Law*; English translation; Oxford, The Clarendon Press, 1925).

[3] Francisci de Victoria, *De indis et de iure belli relectiones*, 1696 edition, (*The Classics of International Law*; English translation; Washington, The Carnegie Institution, 1917).

[4] On the influence of these Spaniards see: Arthur Nussbaum, *A Concise History*

though divided into different nations and states, still has a certain unity, not only as a species but, as it were, politically and morally as is indicated by the precept of mutual love and charity which extends to all, even to strangers of any nation whatsoever. Therefore, though each perfect polity, republic, or kingdom is in itself a perfect community, consisting of its members, nevertheless each of these communities, inasmuch as it is related to the human race, is in a sense also a member of this universal society. Never, indeed, are these communities, singly, so self-sufficient unto themselves as not to need a certain mutual aid and association and communications, sometimes for their welfare and advantage, sometimes because of a moral necessity or indigence, as experience shows. For this reason they need a law by which they are guided and rightly ordered in respect to communication and association. To a great extent this is done by natural reason but not so sufficiently and directly everywhere. Hence, certain special rules could be established by the customs of these nations [5].

On the other hand the protestant Italo-Englishman, ALBERICO GENTILI [6] (1552–1608), though certainly not an opponent of the idea of natural law, wrote in more of a secular vein and tended to rely more on the practices of international affairs than on philosophical speculations. Gentili is considered by many to have been the founder of the positivist persuasion [7]. However, it is not completely clear what his philosophical foundations were, as he shows both positivist and naturalist leanings. "It has been made sufficiently clear", says Gentili in a naturalist vein, "that natural law does exist, and that if you should transgress it in any particular, you would desire to conceal the act

of the Law of Nations (New York, The Macmillan Company, 1947), p. 104; Thomas A. Walker, A History of the Law of Nations (Cambridge, Cambridge University Press, 1899), p. 333; James Brown Scott, 'The modern Law of Nations and Its Municipal Sanctions' Georgetown Law Journal (January, 1934), pp. 139–206; James Brown Scott, 'Francisco Suarez His Philosophy of Law and of Sanctions' Georgetown Law Journal (March, 1934), pp. 405–518; James Brown Scott, The Catholic Conception of International Law (Washington, Georgetown University Press, 1934); James Brown Scott, The Spanish Origin of International Law (Oxford, The Clarendon Press, 1934). See also Nussbaum, op. cit., p. 309 for criticism of Scott's works.

[5] Nussbaum, op. cit., p. 67.

[6] Alberico Gentili, De iure belli libri tres, 1612 edition, 2 vols. (The Classics Of International Law; English translation; Oxford, The Clarendon Press, 1933).

[7] Nussbaum, op. cit., p. 84 refers to him as "... the originator of the secular school of thought in international law". See also: Thorsten V. Kalijarvi, Modern World Politics (New York, Thomas Y. Crowell Company, 1946), p. 101; John P. Humphry, 'On the Foundations of International Law' The American Journal of International Law, (April, 1945), p. 231.

through very shame [8]." On the other hand, he shows in the following quotation somewhat of a positivist inclination:

For ... [the authors and founders of our laws] say that the law of nations is that which is in use among all the nations of men, which native reason has established among all human beings, and which is equally observed by all mankind. Such law is natural law. 'The agreement of all nations about a matter must be regarded as a law of nature' [9].

All of this, in the eyes of COLEMAN PHILLIPSON (1878–   ) who translated Gentili's work into English and wrote an introduction to it, reduces to the fact that "The law of nations ... is that law which all nations or the greater part of them agree upon [10]." This, in Phillipson's view, is the essence of Gentili's orientation.

Although there has been some dispute about the matter, the preponderance of authority would seem to grant to Hugo Grotius the distinction of having been the real founder of international law in the modern era — "the Father of International Law [11]." To support his views this versatile Dutch jurist drew in particular on the Spanish theologians and on Gentili, and also upon an array of additional classical and ecclesiastical sources.

Grotius' system from the standpoint of philosophy was essentially the same as that of Vitoria and Suárez in that he relied on a natural law superstructure which, however, allowed of a positivist branch subordinate thereto. Grotius drew heavily also from the work of Gentili, especially for documentation. On the philosophical structure of Grotius' work, Lawrence says:

His International Law has two sources, the Law of Nature and the consent of all or of most nations; but the latter is only supplementary to the former and cannot ordain anything contrary to it [12].

---

[8] Gentili, *op. cit.*, p. 10. On Gentili in general see Thomas E. Holland, *Studies in International Law* (Oxford, The Clarendon Press, 1898), pp. 1–39. Nussbaum, *op. cit.*, pp. 75–85.

[9] Gentili, *op. cit.*, p. 8.

[10] *Ibid.*, p. 22a.

[11] Nussbaum, *op. cit.*, p. 107. See also Hamilton Vreeland, *Hugo Grotius* (New York, Oxford University Press, 1917), pp. 235–243. For a somewhat different view see A. P. Sereni, *The Italian Conception of International Law* (New York, Columbia University Press, 1943), pp. 84, 115–116.

[12] Thomas J. Lawrence, *Essays on Some Disputed Questions in Modern International Law* (Cambridge, Deighton Bell and Company, 1885), p. 196.

It must be noted in passing that as far as competence, scope, literary brilliance, tolerance, erudition, or popularity are concerned the precursors of Grotius mentioned above cannot be compared with the famous Dutch master. This is the opinion of the overwhelming majority of scholars [13].

The Englishman, RICHARD ZOUCHE [14] (1590–1660), though greatly influenced by Grotius, followed perhaps more closely in the footsteps of Gentili, in that both relied basically on positivist sources [15]. In view of the confusion surrounding Gentili's works, according to Nussbaum, Zouche may be regarded as the first real positivist [16]. Zouche's own statement is clear and explicit:

Law between nations is the law which is recognized in the community of different princes or peoples who hold sovereign power — that is to say, the law which has been accepted among most nations by customs in harmony with reason, and that upon which single nations agree with one another, and which is observed by nations at peace and by those at war [17].

The positivist influence of Zouche is reflected in the work of SAMUEL RACHEL [18] (1638–1691) who relies for the most part on custom and treaties, while nevertheless recognizing a natural law. He is not clear, however, as to the mutual relationship [19] of these.

This trend toward positivism was continued on into the nineteenth century by CORNELIUS BYNKERSHOEK [20] (1673–1743), JOHANN JAKOB MOSER [21] (1701–1785), and GEORG FRIEDRICH

[13] Nussbaum, *loc. cit.* Also Fenwick, *op. cit.*, p. 51. Also George Grafton Wilson, *International Law* (New York, Silver, Burdett and Company, 1935), pp. 33–34.

[14] Richard Zouche, *Juris et judicii feciales, sive juris inter gentes, et quaestionum de eodem explicatio*, 1650 edition, 2 vols. (*The Classics of International Law*; English translation; Baltimore, The Lord Baltimore Press, 1911).

[15] Nussbaum, *op. cit.*, p. 122.

[16] *Loc. cit.*

[17] Zouche, *op. cit.*, p. 1.

[18] Samuel Rachel, *De jure naturae et gentium dissertationes*, 1676 edition, 2 vols. (*The Classics of International Law*; English translation; Baltimore, The Lord Baltimore Press, 1916).

[19] Nussbaum, *op. cit.*, pp. 122–125.

[20] Cornelius van Bynkershoek, *Quaestionum juris publici libri duo*, 1737 edition, 2 vols. (*The Classics of International Law*; English translation; Oxford, The Clarendon Press, 1930).

[21] Johann Jakob Moser, *Versuch des neuesten europaischen Volkerrechts in Friedens- und Kriegszeiten, vornehmlich aus denen Staatshandlungen derer europaischen Machten, auch anderen Begebenheiten, so sich seit dem Tode Kaiser Karls VI im Jahre 1740 zugetragen haben*, 10 vols. (Frankfurt am Mayn, Varrentrapp sohn und Wenner, 1777–80).

VON MARTENS [22] (1756–1821). The first of these three relied on reason, treaties, and custom. Reason, in Bynkershoek's view, rather than being scholastic or dogmatic in character, amounted to a form of common sense which was embodied in treaties and usages. These last two, however, were conceived of as being the most important factors in international law and, consequently, the positivist tendency is manifest [23]. Similarly, the work of Moser represents an attempt to rely almost exclusively on treaties and customs [24]. That of Martens follows in the same general tradition although he recognizes natural law elements to a degree [25], hence leading to a Grotian or neo-Grotian type of juristic thought.

The third major strain of thought which is pertinent to this discussion is the Hobbesian thread of naturalism. Heretofore naturalism had been of importance largely in the Stoic and clerical sense of an ordered scheme of things; under the pen of THOMAS HOBBES [26] (1588–1679) it assumed a very different tack.

Although Hobbes was emphatic in his support of morality, his whole orientation was to the effect that man's first right is self preservation [27], and therefore, this right, as existing in a state of nature where civil government is absent and where the essence of existence is a war of all against all, is regarded as tolerating not the slightest hint of interference. Under civil society this situation no longer obtains. In this regard it is observed that covenants are ineffectual in a state of nature, but not so under civil government. This is because in the former case no power exists to compel both parties to maintain their obligations, while the establishment of civil government provides this power [28]. It is interesting to note that Hobbes' reasoning with respect to the state of nature is that if one party under

[22] Georg Friedrich von Martens, *Précis du droit des gens moderne de l'Europe* (Gottingue, Dieterich, 1801).

[23] Bynkershoek, *op. cit.*, p. 5 et passim. Also Nussbaum, *op. cit.*, p. 144.

[24] Fenwick, *op. cit.*, fn. p. 57. Also Nussbaum, *op. cit.*, p. 166.

[25] Charles Calvo, *Le droit international théorique et pratique* Tomo I (Paris, Guillaumin et Cie., 1887), pp. 70–71. Nussbaum, *op. cit.*, p. 173.

[26] Thomas Hobbes, *Philosophical Rudiments Concerning Government and Society* (in Sir William Molesworth, *The English Works of Thomas Hobbes*, Vol. II, London, John Bohn, 1841).

[27] *Ibid.*, pp. 8–9.

[28] *Ibid.*, pp. 21–22.

a contract anticipates the other party's reciprocation, and if the first party entertains the slightest doubt whether the latter will fulfill his part of the bargain, then, in the state of nature, he is quite justified in not performing in the first place.

As to the mutual relations of states, he considers that these exist in a state of nature and that the condition of *homo homini lupus* obtains in the international sphere. To this effect he says:

But because cities once instituted do put on the personal proprieties of men, that *law*, which speaking of the duty of single men we call *natural*, being applied to whole cities and nations, is called the *right of nations*. And the same elements of *natural law and right*, which have hitherto been spoken of, being transferred to *whole cities* and *nations*, may be taken for the elements of the *laws* and *right of nations* [29].

Hobbes' view is in fact that of a negation of international law, but his influence on such writers as Pufendorf, Spinoza, Austin, James Mill, and Bentham [30] was not insignificant, and therein lies his importance for any survey of the theory of international law.

Although having relatively little to say on this matter, BENEDICT SPINOZA [31] (1632–1677) followed in general the Hobbesian line of thought [32], and from him it was passed on through GEORG WILHELM F. HEGEL (1770–1831) into the nineteenth and twentieth centuries [33] along channels of an ultra-nationalist sort that was to become especially strong in Germany, though certainly not restricted entirely to that country. This strain will be taken up and traced farther at a later moment.

The views of Hobbes exerted considerable influence in England on JOHN AUSTIN (1790–1859), JAMES MILL (1773–1836), and JEREMY BENTHAM (1748–1833) resulting, under the influence of these, in a form of positivism which tended to negate international law as law although it retained in these quarters a moral significance if nothing more [34]. This phase of legal thought

---

[29] *Ibid.*, p. 187.

[30] *Infra* ff. 31, 34, 35, 71 and 72.

[31] Benedict Spinoza, '*Tractatus theologico-politicus*' *The Chief Works of Benedict de Spinoza*, 2 vols. Translated by R. H. M. Elwes. (London, George Bell and Sons, 1883), vol. I, pp. 200–213.

[32] *Loc. cit.* Lauterpacht, 'Spinoza and International Law' *The British Year Book of International Law*, (1927), pp. 89–107.

[33] Lauterpacht, *op. cit.*, pp. 103–104.

[34] George E. Cottin, 'Hobbes, Thomas' *The Encyclopeadia of the Social Sciences*

has been highly influential throughout the nineteenth and twentieth centuries particularly in the English speaking world.

SAMUEL PUFENDORF [35] (1632–1694), who was influenced by both Hobbes and Grotius [36], is credited with being the founder of the natural law school of international law. His denial of the legal validity of positivist elements in international law follows the tradition of Hobbes, but the law of nature, deemed by Pufendorf to be the only legal force among nations, is not the chaotic Hobbesian natural right, but rather an ordered natural law system akin to that of Grotius [37]. The following quotation reflects Pufendorf's views and some of his sources as well:

There is still one question behind, which requires our Determination. Whether or no there be any such thing as a particular and positive *Law of Nations*, contradistinct to the *Law of Nature*. Learned Men are not come to any good Agreement in this Point. Many assert the *Law of Nature and of Nations* to be the very same thing, differing no otherwise than in external Denomination. Thus *Hobbes* divides *Natural Law, into the Natural Law of Men, and the Natural Law of States, commonly called the Law of Nations*. He observes, *That the Precepts of both are the same: But that for as much as States when they are once instituted, assume the Personal Proprieties of Men, hence it comes to pass, that what, speaking of the Duty of particular Men, we call the Law of Nature, the same we term the Law of Nations, when we apply it to whole States, Nations, or People*. This Opinion we, for our part, readily subscribe to: Nor do we conceive, that there is any other Voluntary or Positive Law of Nations, properly invested with a true and legal Force, and obliging as the Ordinance of a Superior Power. And thus we do not really differ in Judgment from those who are more inclin'd to call that the Law of Nature which consists in a Conformity to Rational Nature, and that the Law of Nations, which flows from the Consideration of Human Indigence, the Relief of which seems to be the main end and design of Society. For we,

---

vol. 7, pp. 394–396. Also H. B. Jacobini, 'Some Observations Concerning Jeremy Bentham's Concepts of International Law' *The American Journal of International Law* (April, 1948), pp. 415–417.

[35] Samuel von Pufendorf, *Of the Law of Nature and Nations* (English translation; London, Sare, Bonwicke, Goodwyn, Walthoe, Wotton, *et al.*, 1717). Also S. von Pufendorf, *De officio hominis et civis juxta legem naturalem libri duo*, 1632 edition, 2 vols. (*The Classics of International Law*; English translation; New York, Oxford University Press, 1927).

[36] Fenwick, *op. cit.*, p. 54. Calvo, *op. cit.*, p. 45. Nussbaum, *op. cit.*, p. 116.

[37] Nussbaum, *loc. cit.*

as well as they, deny that there is any positive Law of Nations proceeding from a Superior. And whatever is deducible from Reflections on the Indigence of Human Nature, we refer immediately to *Natural Law*: only we were unwilling to define and explain this Natural Law by a Conformity to Rational Nature; because by this means we should establish Reason for the Rule and Measure of itself; and so this way of demonstrating Nature's Laws would run round in a Circle [38].

How influential Pufendorf may or may not have been is a question of some dispute [39]. However, it seems safe to say that his direct impact on international legal thought was not lasting [40], but that he did have notable influence on non-juristic thinkers like DENYS DIDEROT (1713–1784) and the Encyclopedists and on the enlightenment in general [41]. One of the legal thinkers of the enlightenment who followed in this tradition was CHRISTIAN WOLFF [42] (1676–1756), a student of GOTTFRIED WILHELM LEIBNITZ (1646–1716). Instead of developing a pure natural law system, Wolff evolved a four-fold arrangement built around his conception of the *civitas maxima*, the essence of which was a sort of understanding or pact — Nussbaum suggests that it might be characterized as "subconscious" [43] regarded as existing among the nations. The body of reasoned rules drawn from this *civitas maxima* he called the *jus voluntarium*, but although they were regarded as based on natural law, at the same time they were seen as distinct from the *jus necessarium* which meant the pure law of nature. In addition, he recognized in customs and treaties a third and a fourth category of law. As also in Grotius' system, the *jus necessarium* held the favored place in the hierarchy [44].

Wolff's influence probably would not have been considerable

---

[38] Pufendorf, *Of the Law of Nature and Nations*, Book II, pp. 149–150.

[39] Fenwick, *loc. cit.*

[40] According to Fenwick, f. *loc. cit.*, only a very few publicists have followed Pufendorf. Among these were Christian Thomasius (1655–1728), Jean Barbeyrac (1674–1744), Jean Jacques Burlamiqui (1694–1784), Thomas Rutherforth (1712–71), and James Lorimer (1818–90).

[41] Chester C. Maxey, Political Philosophies (New York, The Macmillan Company, 1948), p. 300. Nussbaum, *op. cit.*, pp. 148–163. Also Fenwick, *op. cit.*, pp. 54–55.

[42] Christian von Wolff, *Jus gentium methodo scientifica pertractatum*, 1764 edition, 2 vols. (*The Classics of International Law*; English translation; Oxford, The Clarendon Press, 1934).

[43] Nussbaum, *op. cit.*, p. 151.

[44] *Ibid.*, pp. 151–152.

had it not been for his illustrious pupil, EMER DE VATTEL [45] (1741–1767), whose work, *The Law of Nations or the Principles of Natural Law Applied to the Conduct of the Affairs of Nations and of Sovereigns*, was to meet with great favor. Although most contemporary writers seem to feel that Vattel's good fortune exceeded the intrinsic merit of his work [46], he was destined to have wide influence [47]. Vattel's philosophy of the law of nations was much like that of his teacher, Wolff, except that he omitted the concept of the *civitas maxima*. His system embraced four types of law, *necessary law* which nations are bound to observe because of its innate and obvious justness, *voluntary law*, also based on natural law but composed of rules which because of the uncertainness of the dictates of natural law each state would determine for itself, *treaty law*, and *customary law*. The necessary or natural law was considered as situate at the top of the hierarchy [48].

By this tortuous route, then, the naturalist strain entered the general stream of nineteenth century philosophy of international law.

From the foregoing sketch it may be seen that the late eighteenth and early nineteenth century philosophy of international law included three major points of view called, still, by the names positivist, naturalist, and Grotian, but each representing a somewhat different outlook from that of its terminological predecessor. These were: a Grotian view represented by Vattel and by Martens which had not only early Grotian, but also positivist, and naturalist antecedents; an English positivist view stemming from Hobbes and best seen in the works of Bentham and Austin who denied the legal validity of international law; and a German naturalist conception stemming also from Hobbes but via Spinoza and Hegel.

---

[45] Emir de Vattel, *Le droit des gens, ou principes de la loi naturelle, appliqués à la conduite et aux affaires des nations et des souverains*, 3 vols. (*The Classics of International Law*; English translation; Washington, The Carnegie Institution, 1916).
[46] Nussbaum, *op. cit.*, p. 160. Pittman B. Potter, *A Manual Digest of Common International Law* (New York, Harper and Brothers, 1932), p. 120.
[47] Fenwick, *op. cit.*, p. 56.
[48] Vattel, *op. cit.*, p. 9. Also Fenwick, *op. cit.*, pp. 55–56.

Although the basic thought of international law throughout the nineteenth and twentieth centuries is generally characterized as emphasizing positivism, there was at least one important and highly influential naturalist thread which deserves considerable attention, *i.e.*, the view spoken of by some writers as the school of force. In addition, the so-called nationality school, or Italian school, of international law may be treated here under the same general head, *i.e.*, as a form of naturalism.

In the nineteenth century the influence of Hegel and consequently the conceptions of Hobbes and Spinoza were felt throughout the world, but especially in Germany. The German anti-semitic historian, HEINREICH VON TREITSCHKE [49] (1834–1896), emphasized that the nature of the state and of international relations is such that binding international law is an impossibility. His statement including a glorification of war is a classic which perhaps better than any other sets in relief this Germanic concept.

We have described the State as an independent force. This pregnant theory of independence implies firstly so absolute a moral supremacy that the State cannot legitimately tolerate any power above its own, and secondly a temporal freedom entailing a variety of material resources adequate to its protection against hostile influences. Legal sovereignty, the State's complete independence of any other earthly power, is so rooted in its nature that it may be said to be its very standard and criterion . . . .

Human communities do exist which in their own fashion pursue aims no less lofty than those of the State, but which must be legally subject to it in their own outward relations with the world. It is obvious that contradictions must arise, and that two such authorities, morally but not legally equal, must sometimes collide with each other. Nor is it to be wished that the conflicts between Church and State should wholly cease, for if they did one party or the other would be soulless and dead, like the Russian Church for example. Sovereignty, however, which is the peculiar attribute of the State, is of necessity supreme, and it is a ridiculous inconsistency to speak of a superior and inferior authority within it. The truth remains that the essence of the State consists in its incompatibility

---

[49] Heinrich von Treitschke, 'Politics' *Introduction to Contemporary Civilization in the West*, Vol. II (New York, Columbia University Press, 1946).

with any power over it. How proudly and truly statesmanlike is Gustavus Adolphus' exclamation, "I recognize no power over me but God and the conqueror's sword". This is so unconditionally true that we see at once that it cannot be the destiny of mankind to form a single State, but that the ideal towards which we strive is a harmonious comity of nations, who, concluding treaties of their own free will, admit restrictions upon their sovereignty without abrogating it.

For the notion of sovereignty must not be rigid, but flexible and relative, like all political conceptions. Every State, in treaty making, will limit its power in certain directions for its own sake. States which conclude treaties with each other thereby curtail their absolute authority to some extent. But the rule still stands, for every treaty is a voluntary curb upon the power of each, and all international agreements are prefaced by the clause "Rebus sic stantibus". No State can pledge its future to another. It knows no arbiter, and draws up all its treaties with this implied reservation. This is supported by the axiom that so long as international law exists all treaties lose their force at the very moment when war is declared between the contracting parties; moreover, every sovereign State has the undoubted right to declare war at its pleasure, and is consequently entitled to repudiate its treaties. Upon this constantly recurring alteration of treaties the progress of history depends; every State must take care that its treaties do not survive their effective value, lest another Power should denounce them by a declaration of war; for antiquated treaties must necessarily be denounced and replaced by others more consonant with circumstances.

It is clear that the international agreements which limit the power of a State are not absolute, but voluntary self-restrictions. Hence, it follows that the establishment of a permanent international Arbitration Court is incompatable with the nature of the State, which could at all events only accept the decision of such a tribunal in cases of second- or third-rate importance. When a nation's existence is at stake there is no outside Power whose impartiality can be trusted. Were we to commit the folly of treating the Alsace-Lorraine problem as an open question, by submitting it to arbitration, who would seriously believe that the award could be impartial? It is, moreover, a point of honour for a State to solve such difficulties for itself. International treaties may indeed become more frequent, but a finally decisive tribunal of the nations is an impossibility. The appeal to arms will be valid until the end of history, and therein lies the sacredness of war [50].

---

[50] *Ibid.*, pp. 769–770.

In virtually the same vein a number of German juristic thinkers subscribed to the so-called principle of "auto-limitation" [51] which seems to be little more than a watered version of the above from Treitschke with an added touch of magnanimity. These writers, among whom GEORG JELLINEK [52] (1851–1911) and RUDOLF VON JHERING [53] (1818–1892) stand out prominently, viewed all international law as being based on treaties (actual treaties or as tacitly implied in customs) and hence on the consent of states — a consent which could be legally revoked but which would normally be allowed to stand [54]. An even more emphatic statement of this view was that made by ERICH KAUFMANN [55] (1880–   ) in which on the basis of the *clausula rebus sic stantibus* [56] he negates international law entirely [57].

In the modern period the National Socialists in Germany attempted to make use of international law in pursuit of certain of their aims. Their's was a naturalistic approach which sought to justify, often in racist terms, a defense of the fundamental right of the state to independence, self preservation, self development, living space, *etc.*, in other words to justify an all embracing state sovereignty. Regarding ethnic considerations it sought to justify racism in terms of the right of the nordics to rule [58].

Through these channels, then, the Germanic thread of Hobbesian naturalism has come down to the present time.

---

[51] Jean Spiropoulos, *Théorie générale du droit international* (Paris, Librairie générale de droit & de jurisprudence, 1930), pp. 45–52.

[52] Georg Jellinek, *Der rechtliche Natur der Staatenvertrage* (Wien, A. Holder, 1880).

[53] Rudolf von Jhering, *Law as an End in Itself* (The Modern Legal Philosophy Series, vol. V; Boston, The Boston Book Company, 1913).

[54] Fenwick, *op. cit.*, p. 59.

[55] Erich Kaufmann, *Das Wesen des Volkerrechts und die clausula rebus sic stantibus* (Tübingen, J. C. B. Mohr, 1911).

[56] On the *clausula rebus sic stantibus* see: Chesney Hill, *The Doctrine of Rebus Sic Stantibus* (Columbia, The University of Missouri, 1934); H. Lauterpacht, *The Function of Law in the International Community* (Oxford, Oxford University Press, 1933), pp. 270–285 *et passim*; Eduardo Jimenez de Arechaga, 'Existencia y caracter juridico del derecho internacional publico' *Revista de derecho internacional* Tomo LVII, pp. 205–207.

[57] Fenwick, *loc. lit.*

[58] Joseph Florin and John H. Herz, 'Bolshevist and National Socialist Doctrines of International Law' *Social Research*, (February, 1940), pp. 1–31. Also John H. Herz, 'The National Socialist Doctrine of International Law and the Problems of International Organization' *Political Science Quarterly*, (December, 1939), pp. 536–554. Also Nussbaum, *op. cit.*, pp. 278–280.

Another approach to international law which may seem, superficially at least, to be related to the Germanic theory of state sovereignty is the so-called Italian conception of international law [59]. This view sprang from the impelling desire of the Italians for national unity. It appears as the legal counterpart of GIUSEPPI MAZZINI's (1805–1872) justification of the nation-state as the medium through which the individual can make his contribution to humanity at large [60].

This legal conception was first set forth by PASQUALE STANISLAO MANCINI [61] (1817–1888), who, in 1850 at the University of Turin delivered an inaugural lecture entitled "Nationality as the Basis of the Law of Nations." Mancini emphasized the right of each nationality to organize as an independent state [62]. Apparently the chief imprint of this point of view has been in the realm of private international law in which various states have enacted legislation designed to direct their courts, when dealing with foreigners in respect to such matters as divorce, marriage, and inheritance, to apply the law of the litigants' nationality and not the law of their domicile [63].

The Italian conception of international law has never developed notions of state or race glorification; rather it has reflected a view akin to that of the Wilsonian concept of self-determination [64].

In this rapid survey a word might be inserted regarding the Soviet conception of the law of nations [65]. Under the Soviet

---

[59] Angelo Piero Sereni, *The Italian Conception of International Law* (New York, Columbia University Press, 1943), pp. 155–181. Also Alesandro Levi, 'Mancini, Pasquale Staneslao' *The Encyclopaedia of the Social Sciences*, vol. 10, p. 84. Also Nussbaum, *op. cit.*, pp. 225–228.

[60] Joseph Mazzini, 'Duties Toward Your Country' *Introduction to Contemporary Civilization in the West*, vol. II, p. 346.

[61] Pasquale Stanislao Mancini, 'Della nazionalità come fondamento del diritto delle gendi' *Diritto internazionale* (Roma, Unione Tip. Manuzio, 1905). See also Sereni, *op. cit.*, p. 161 where it is suggested that these two men arrived at similar conclusions independently.

[62] Sereni, *op. cit.*, pp. 162–164. Levi, *loc. cit.* Also Nussbaum, *op. cit.*, p. 226.

[63] Nussbaum, *op. cit.*, pp. 226–227, also Sereni, *op. cit.*, pp. 177–178 *et passim*.

[64] Both of these points of view stress the nation rather than the state, and both have tended to be oriented toward peace.

[65] Timothy A. Taracouzio, *The Soviet Union and International Law* (New York, The Macmillan Company, 1935); also Rudolf Schlesinger, *Soviet Legal Theory* (London, Kega Paul et al., 1946), pp. 273–290; also John N. Hazard, 'Cleansing Soviet International Law of Anti-Marxist Theories' *The American Journal of International Law*, (April, 1938), pp. 244–252. Also Eugene A. Korovin, 'The Second World War and International Law' *The American Journal of International Law*, (October,

government, international law has undergone several changes in which various authors, who for a time seemed to express "true doctrine", at a later date were forced to recant and confess error. Soviet practice has been highly opportunistic. The Russians themselves profess to have used the idea of a transition international law simply as an expedient to help regulate international relations through the "transition period" of Soviet-Western adjustment [66]. According to Nussbaum,

Recent Soviet writers agree that international law consists of two heterogeneous parts: one of bourgeois and the other of Soviet origin, the former composed of the more liberal rules not incompatible with Soviet principles [67].

YEVGENY ALEXANDROVITCH KOROVIN (1892–   ), one of the leading contemporary Russian writers and authorities on international law, is quoted by Chakste as follows:

Like any other law, international law reflects the will of the ruling classes. The reality of international law, however, is not precluded by the fact that for the time being there are on the international stage bourgeois states as well as feudal and socialist ones. Each of them, carrying out its own line and directed by its own motives, might be interested in supporting and preserving a certain amount of generally binding legal norms in international relations [68].

There seems to be much evidence to support the view that Soviet international law is, at best, a highly ephemeral phenomenon [69].

Another relatively recent movement in the realm of legal philosophy is the so-called American school of international law. It is mentioned at this point, however, only to acknowledge its existence among other particularist points of view, since a survey of its principal features will comprise a somewhat extensive study later in this work [70].

1946), pp. 742–755. Also see *Infra*, ff. 66 and 67. For Russian sources see especially the works of Korovin and Pashukanis. For periodic Comments see W. W. Kulski, in *American Journal of International Law* (1951, 1952 and 1953).

[66] Taracouzio, *op. cit.*, pp. 10–11 *et passim*.

[67] Nussbaum, *op. cit.*, pp. 290–291.

[68] Mentauts Chakste, 'Soviet Concepts of the State, International Law and Sovereignty' *The American Journal of International Law*, (January, 1949), p. 30.

[69] *Loc. cit.* Florin and Herz, *op. cit.*, pp. 27–31 *et passim*.

[70] See chapter 4 of this work.

As was observed earlier, the dominant ethos throughout the nineteenth and early twentieth centuries, as far as international law is concerned, was that of positivism. This does not mean that the concepts of equity, natural reason, and ethical moralistic naturalism were not part of this thread, but they tended, on the whole, to play subsidiary roles.

The viewpoint of the *analytical* jurists in general was that, while denying international law as law, they recognized it as positive morality [71]. Some of the writers of this tradition, however, viewed the matter somewhat differently. JAMES MILL (1773–1836), for example, took the position that international law was in fact true law, which rested on the sanction of world public opinion [72]. Whether law "properly so-called" or merely positive morality, however, international law in their eyes was in any case a positive phenomenon.

Also the jurists of the *historical* school were strong positivists. This school, represented notably by FRIEDRICH KARL VON SAVIGNY [73] (1779–1861) and SIR HENRY JAMES SUMNER MAINE [74] (1822–1888), emphasized the place of custom in law. It was maintained by these thinkers that if a rule were recognized and observed, this made it law, and that the *enacted* law which Austin had emphasized had appeared on the legal horizon in relatively recent time. Logically, therefore, historicism viewed international law as true law.

The great bulk of the thinkers who were concerned with the subject of international law throughout this period cannot, however, as a general rule be classified either as analytical or historical jurists *per se*, but rather, either as Grotians or as

---

[71] John Austin, *Lectures on Jurisprudence* 2 vols., (New York, James Cockcroft and Company, 1875), vol. I, pp. 121–122, vol. II, p. 177. Also Jeremy Bentham, *The Works of Jeremy Bentham* (Published under the superintendence of his executor, John Bowring, Edinburgh, William Tait, 1843. Vol. III), p. 162. See also H. B. Jacobini, *loc. cit.*

[72] James Mill, 'Law of Nations' *Selected Writings* (of Jeremy Bentham, James Mill, and John Stuart Mill) (Garden City, Doubleday Doran and Company, Inc., 1935), pp. 285–290.

[73] Friedrich K. von Savigny, *Of the Vocation of Our Age for Legislation and Jurisprudence* (English translation; London, Littlewood and Company, 1831).

[74] Henry Sumner Maine, *International Law* (New York, Henry Holt and Company, 1888). Also H. S. Maine, *Ancient Law* (New York, Henry Holt and Company, 1879).

positivists in the sense in which Mosier is called a positivist in that the latter considered international law to be based almost exclusively on treaties and customs. Another distinction which needs to be kept in mind regarding the writers of this period is that they were sometimes split along Anglo-American versus Continental lines, each following the penchant of its own juristic tradition of domestic law [75]. Although there were numerous writers who with some degree of success bridged this gap, among whom HENRY WHEATON [76] (1785–1848) and later LASSA FRANCES LAWRENCE OPPENHEIM [77] (1858–1919) were perhaps the best examples, the divergence of method between these groups has led them to be referred to as the Anglo-American and Continental schools with stress respectively upon cases and precedents and on the other hand upon abstract theories [78].

Some of the outstanding publicists of the period were: JOHANN LUDWIG KLÜBER [79] (1762–1837) who emphasized positive law but thought to fill its gaps with resort to natural law [80]; AUGUST WILHELM HEFFTER [81] (1796–1880) who relied entirely on customs and treaties [82]; and HEINRICH TRIEPEL [83] (1868–1946) who emphasized agreements between states [84]. Among the British, Sir ROBERT JOSEPH PHILLIMORE (1810–1885), though recognizing natural law elements emphasized custom and treaty law [85]; WILLIAM EDWARD HALL (1835–1894) emphasized positivism

---

[75] Alejandro Alvarez, 'The New International Law' *Transactions of the Grotius Society*, (1930), p. 43. Also Nussbaum, *op. cit.*, pp. 276–278. For an opposite view see H. Lauterpacht, 'The So-Called Anglo-American and Continental Schools of Thought in International Law' *The British Year Book of International Law*, (1931), pp. 31–62.

[76] Henry Wheaton, *Elements of International Law* (Boston, Little Brown and Company, 1863).

[77] L. Oppenheim, *International Law A Treatise*, 2nd edition, 2 vols. (London, Longmans Green and Company, 1912).

[78] Nussbaum, *op. cit.*, pp. 234, 277.

[79] Johann Ludwig Klüber, *Droit des gens moderne de l'Europe*, 2 vols. (Stuttgart, J. G. Cotta, 1819).

[80] Fenwick, *op. cit.*, p. 59.

[81] August Wilhelm Heffter, *Das europaische Volkerrecht der gegenwart* (Berlin, E. H. Schroeder, 1844).

[82] Nussbaum, *op. cit.*, p. 230.

[83] Heinrich Triepel, *Droit international et droit interne* (Paris, A. Pedone, 1920).

[84] Triepel, *op. cit.*, pp. 27–61. Fenwick, *loc. cit.*

[85] Robert Joseph Phillimore, *Commentaries Upon International Law* vol. I (Philadelphia, T. and J. W. Johnson, Law Booksellers, 1854), pp. 55–91 especially pp. 55, 64–69, and 86.

throughout [86]; L. Oppenheim, THOMAS JOSEPH LAWRENCE [87] (1849–1920) and, among the Americans, Henry Wheaton, JAMES KENT [88] (1763–1847) and the successors of these followed much the same line of thought, *i.e.*, the basic theme was positivistic but with some acknowledgment at times of naturalistic elements [89].

The movement toward positivism did not, by any means, wipe out in its entirety the natural law tradition. In France particularly, but elsewhere as well, some publicists have persisted in variations of this view. Such writers as PAUL LOUIS ERNEST PRADIER-FODÉRÉ [90] (1827–1904), PASUQALE FIORE [91] (1837–1914), and later LOUIS ÉRASME LE FUR [92] (1870–1943), emphasized abstract principles [93]. In very recent years the writings of HERSH LAUTERPACHT [94] (1897–   ) have stressed elements of this tradition.

There were, during this period, a few attempts on the part of individual jurists to write codes of international law. Among the most notable are those of JOHANN KASPAR BLUNTSCHLI [95] (1808–1881), DAVID DUDLY FIELD [96] (1805–1894), Pasquale Fiore [97], and LEONE LEVI [98] (1821–1888).

The practices of states were emphasized by such works as

---

[86] William Edward Hall, *A Treatise on International Law* 4th edition (London, The Clarendon Press, 1895), pp. 1–2.

[87] Thomas J. Lawrence, *Principles of International Law*, 3rd edition (Boston, Little, Brown, and Company, 1900).

[88] James Kent, *Commentaries on American Law I* (Boston, Little, Brown and Company, 1896), pp. 2–3.

[89] Fenwick, *op. cit.*, pp. 57–59.

[90] Paul L. E. Pradiere-Fodéré, *Traité de droit international public européen et américain* 8 vols. (Paris, G. Pedone-Lauriel, 1885–1906).

[91] Pasquale Fiore, *Trattado di diritto internazionale pubblico* 3 vols. (Torino, Unione tipografico, 1887–91). Also P. Fiore, *International Law Codified and Its Legal Sanction* (New York, Baker, Voorhis and Company, 1918).

[92] Louis E. Le Fur, *Précis de droit international public* (Paris, Librairie Dalloz, 1933).

[93] Calvo, *op. cit.*, p. 153. Also Nussbaum, *op. cit.*, pp. 230–231. Also Fenwick, *op. cit.*, p. 60. Also Fiore, *International Law Codified*, pp. 90–91, and 94–95.

[94] H. Lauterpacht, *International Law and Human Rights* (New York, Frederick A. Praeger, Inc., 1950).

[95] Johann Kaspar Bluntschli, *Das moderne Völkerrecht der civilisirten Staaten als Rechtsbuch dargestellt* (Nordlingen, C. H. Beck, 1878).

[96] David Dudley Field, *Draft Outlines of an International Code* 2 vols. (New York, Diossy and Company, 1872).

[97] *Supra* fn. 90.

[98] Leone Levi, *International Law with Materials for a Code of International Law* (New York, D. Appleton and Company, 1888).

FRANCIS WHARTON'S [99] (1820–1889) *Digest of the International Law of the United States*, and, in Latin America, RAFAEL FERNANDO SEIJAS' (1822–1901 supposed) somewhat similar compendium [100].

In general these nineteenth century movements have carried on into the twentieth century wherein notable examples of each might be cited. Such compendia of state practices as JOHN BASSETT MOORE's [101] (1860–1947) *A Digest of International Law*, and GREEN HAYWOOD HACKWORTH's [102] (1883–   ) *Digest of International Law*, also texts and treatises such as those by CHARLES GHEQUIERE FENWICK [103] (1880–   ), GEORGE GRAFTON WILSON [104] (1863–1951), and CHARLES CHENEY HYDE [105] (1873–1952) in the United States, and in England those of JAMES LESLIE BRIERLY [106] (1881–   ) together with revisions of Oppenheim [107] and Hall [108], these followed the positivist tradition. Also numerous attempts at codification were made, and some of these, such as the Bustamente Code, were enacted into law. In this last mentioned category one might cite the numerous multilateral conventions such as those resulting from the Hague conferences of 1899 [109] and 1907 [110] and, again, the Civil Aviation Convention of 1945 [111], to mention only a few.

Perhaps the best way to characterize the now current conception of the origin and sources of international law is to turn to the Statute of the World Court which appears to reflect a most happy union of divergent concepts. This amalgamation

---

[99] Frances Wharton, *A Digest of the International Law of the United States* 3 vols. (Washington, Government Printing Office, 1886).

[100] Rafael Fernando Seijas, *El derecho internacional hispano americano* 6 vols. (Caracas, Imprenta de 'El Monitor', 1884).

[101] John Bassett Moore, *A Digest of International Law* 8 vols. (Washington, Government Printing Office, 1906).

[102] Green Haywood Hackworth, *Digest of International Law* 8 vols. (Washington, Government Printing Office, 1940–44).

[103] *Supra* fn. 1.

[104] *Supra* fn. 13.

[105] Charles Cheney Hyde, *International Law Chiefly as Interpreted and Applied by the United States* 3 vols. (Boston, Little, Brown and Company, 1947).

[106] James Leslie Brierly, The Law of Nations (Oxford, The Clarendon Press, 1949).

[107] L. Oppenheim, *op. cit.*, 1948, 7th edition. (edited by H. Lauterpacht).

[108] William Edward Hall, *op. cit.*, 1917, 7th edition (edited by A. P. Higgins).

[109] *The Proceedings of the Hague Peace Conferences, Conference of 1899*, English translation (New York, Oxford University Press, 1920).

[110] *Proceedings of the Hague Peace Conference, Conference of 1907*, English translation (New York, Oxford University Press, 1920–21).

[111] *International Civil Aviation Conference* (Washington, United States Government Printing Office, 1945).

might be said to constitute the now predominant view of international law, which, for want of a better term one might call *twentieth century positivistic Grotianism*. It denotes a reliance on treaties and customs without entirely excluding the concepts of equity, reason, common sense, general principles of justice or whatever other guise the concept of natural law as a moderator of law might take.

Article 38 of the Statute of the International Court of Justice exemplifies this general agreement in the following terms:

1. The Court, whose function is to decide in accordance with international law such disputes as are submitted to it, shall apply:
   a. international conventions, whether general or particular, establishing rules expressly recognized by the contesting states;
   b. international custom, as evidence of a general practice accepted as law;
   c. the general principles of law recognized by civilized nations;
   d. subject to the provisions of Article 59, judicial decisions and the teachings of the most highly qualified publicists of the various nations, as subsidiary means for the determination of rules of law.
2. This provision shall not prejudice the power of the Court to decide a case *ex aequo et bono*, if the parties agree thereto [112]
.

Although the dilemma established by the incompatible coexistence of national sovereignty and international law had earlier been partially resolved by such rigidly logical expedients as Austinianism and the doctrine of auto-limitation, the fundamental fact remained that international law was a force which could not be written off as entirely subordinate to state whim, while at the same time the concept of national sovereignty could not be easily sidestepped.

In answer to this state of affairs two general theoretical approaches developed. Most writers took a more or less traditional view and became known as "dualists", while another

---

[112] *Statute of the International Court of Justice*, Article 38. Article 59 which is mentioned in Article 38 reads as follows: "The decision of the Court has no binding force except between parties and in respect of that particular case". For an explanation of the term 'general principles of law' see Josef L. Kunz, 'The Meaning and the Range of the Norm *Pacta Sunt Servanda*' *The American Journal of International Law*, (April, 1945), pp. 190–192.

group assumed what came to be known as the "monist" view [113]. The dualists, among whom Heinrich Triepel [114] and DIONISIO ANZILOTTI [115] (1869–1950) have been the outstanding continental exponents, held to the persuasion that international law and municipal law are basically of different kind, functioning upon separate premises, and that each is the result of agreement within its own sphere, the former from inter-statal accords, and the latter from agreement within a given state. According to this view, international law would have to be enacted or otherwise absorbed into municipal law before it could be enforced as such, and vice versa [116]. According to Anzilotti, treaty law was based on the norm *pacta sunt servanda* [117] which was not subject to legal analysis, while domestic law is binding "... by virtue of the rule which imposes obedience to the commandments of the legislature ... [118]."

In England and the United States numerous writers have assumed very much this same point of view under what has normally been called the doctrine of "incorporation". W. W. WILLOUGHBY (1867–1945) takes this position when he observes that if national courts enforce a rule of international law, it is enforced as municipal law [119]. JAMES W. GARNER (1871–1938), although he grudgingly concedes the point, observes that "The theory of 'acceptance and adoption', it must be admitted, is probably in accord with the practice of states [120]." International law, he would say, is still *inter*-national and not *supra*-national, for,

...the supremacy of international law does not exist in the sense that national courts may disregard the law of their own

[113] J. G. Starke, 'Monism and Dualism in the Theory of International Law' *The British Year Book of International Law* (1936), pp. 66–81. It must be pointed out that the terms dualist and monist are used here in a purely judicial sense. These terms must not be confused with the words pluralist and monist as applied to the question of internal sovereignty.

[114] *Supra*, fn. 83.

[115] Dionisio Anzilotti, *Cours de droit international* (Paris, Recueil Sirey, 1929).

[116] Nussbaum, *op. cit.*, pp. 281–282.

[117] On this principle see Kunz, *op. cit.*, pp. 180–197. Also Humphry, *op. cit.*, pp. 231–243.

[118] Anzilotti, *op. cit.*, pp. 53, 69; also cf. Spiropoulos, *op. cit.*, pp. 72–76. On the whole subject of dualism see Anzilotti, pp. 49–65.

[119] W. W. Willoughby, 'The Legal Nature of International Law' *The American Journal of International Law*, (April, 1908), p. 365 *et passim*.

[120] James W. Garner, *Recent Developments in International Law* (Calcutta, The University of Calcutta, 1925), p. 7.

state when in their opinion it is repugnant to the prescriptions of international law [121].

This, he hastens to add, does not give a state the right to enact legislation contrary to international law, but merely points up the obligation of the national courts to enforce domestic law internally regardless of the dictates of international law [122]. Besides these there are a great many others of the same persuasion among whom are James L. Brierly [123] in England, and EDWIN D. DICKENSON [124] (1887–   ), QUINCY WRIGHT [125] (1890–   ), and Charles G. Fenwick [126] in the United States.

This doctrine, thoroughly embedded in the Anglo-American legal tradition, can be seen in its fullest extent in the English case of Mortensen v. Peters [127] in which a Norwegian was convicted in the Scottish High Court of Justiciary of fishing in an area which, while outside the three mile limit, had been proscribed by act of parliament. The court made the following clear cut statement:

In this court we have nothing to do with the question of whether the Legislature has or has not done what foreign powers may consider a usurpation in a question with them. Neither are we a tribunal sitting to decide whether an act of the legislature is *ultra vires* as in contravention of generally acknowledged principles of international law. For us an Act of Parliament duly passed by Lords and Commons and assented to by the King, is supreme, and we are bound to give effect to its terms [128].

This does not imply that the issue of necessity ends with the court decision. The obligation still stands as between states irrespective of what may obtain internally. In the case mentioned above the executive remitted the fine in conformity with England's obligations under international law [129].

This general viewpoint, whether termed the dualist conception

[121] *Ibid.*, p. 11.
[122] *Ibid.*, p. 12.
[123] Brierly, *op. cit.*, pp. 77–84.
[124] Edwin D. Dickinson, 'Changing Concepts and the Doctrine of Incorporation' *The American Journal of International Law* (April, 1932), p. 260.
[125] Quincy Wright, 'International Law in Its Relation to Constitutional Law' *The American Journal of International Law*, (April, 1923), p. 244.
[126] Fenwick, *op. cit.*, pp. 87–97.
[127] 14 Scots L. T. R. 227 (1906). Also Charles G. Fenwick, *Cases on International Law*. (Chicago, Callaghan and Company, 1935), pp. 25–28.
[128] Fenwick, *ibid.*, p. 26.
[129] *Ibid.*, fn., p. 28.

of law or the doctrine of incorporation, is in practice that which states have tended to act upon, and it is related closely to the notion of national sovereignty with all the unfortunate ramifications of that conception. It is not odd, then, that dissatisfaction with the international *status quo*, including the dualist-incorporationist thesis, came to be asserted by international law writers as well as by many who were interested in international relations from a non-juridical point of view.

The most important malcontents among legal thinkers are those who, while representative of several differing viewpoints, are all known as monists with regard to their consideration of all juridical law as constituting a sort of universal web rather than under the two separate categories of international law and domestic law. It will perhaps suffice to mention, among these, the three best known views [130] together with certain concepts which are perhaps less well-known but which seem to this writer to be significant.

The Dutch legal thinker, HUGO KRABBE (1859–1936) conceived of law as sovereign even over states. The rules of law, in his view, whether domestic or international represent a consensus of what is just in a sense that may be regarded as recognizable by the innate psychological faculty of man [131]. Accordingly, the basic conception of both international and domestic law would be essentially the same, hence the "monist" designation. Krabbe considers that, in the relationship between the two, the norms of international law take priority as having the wider scope [132].

HANS KELSEN [133] (1883–   ) is the founder of the "pure theory of law" or the "Vienna school". His system, in some respects like Austin's, but more all-embracing [134], is based on the

---

[130] Walter E. Sandelius, 'The Question of Sovereignty and Recent Trends of Juristic Thought' *Twentieth Century Political Thought*, edited by J. S. Roucek (New York, Philosophical Library, 1946), pp. 159–168. Also Nussbaum, *op. cit.*, pp. 283–287.

[131] Hugo Krabbe, *The Modern Idea of the State* (New York, D. Appleton and Company, 1922), pp. 83–90 and 236.

[132] *Ibid.*, p. 247. Also Nussbaum, *op. cit.*, pp. 283–284.

[133] Hans Kelsen, *General Theory of Law and State* (Cambridge, Harvard University Press, 1945).

[134] Sandelius, *op. cit.*, p. 152. Also Lon L. Fuller, *The Problems of Jurisprudence* (Brooklyn, The Foundation Press, Inc., 1949), pp. 109–113.

fundamental postulate that international legal custom is binding [135] as such, hence the binding nature of general international law including the principle, *pacta sunt servanda*. General international law also gives validity to national constitutions that in turn validate national laws, and so on down the line [136]. In as much as the system of legal norms embraces all levels of law, this, like Krabbe's conception, is usually called "monist".

The French writer, LEON DUGUIT (1859–1929) represents a highly influential line of thought which considers law as emanating from a sentiment of social solidarity which determines the rules of law and causes them to be enforced [137]. Of this view Bonnard says:

These rules, beginning as mere social rules, develop into rules of law when "the man of individual consciousness" considers it necessary to assure their observance by a socially organized sanction. The primary fact in the realm of law therefore is not subjective right but the objective rule of law springing from social relationships. This conception led Duguit to reject the German theory of law as a creation of the state, a sovereignty subject only to its own limitations. He insisted that experience shows law to be anterior and external to the state, which because of its nature may itself be limited by law [138].

This sociological conception of law has won quite a following throughout the western world [139]. Its influence in Latin America has been notable, as will be observed in considerable detail at a later point in this study.

In addition to the three well-known points of view outlined above, a degree of completeness would seem to require mention also of the French writer, Louis Le Fur [140], who similarly took a monist position, but who, in so doing, followed the naturalist idea to the extent of observing that international law was merely a manifestation of natural law [141].

[135] Kelsen, *op. cit.*, pp. 369–370.
[136] *Ibid.*, pp. 366–368.
[137] Leon Duguit, 'Objective Law', *Columbia Law Review*, XX, XXI (Dec., 1920, Jan., Feb., & March, 1921) (Translated by Margaret Grandgent. Also Leon Duguit, *Law in the Modern State* (New York, B. W. Huebsch, 1919), pp. 69–72.
[138] Roger Bonnard, 'Duguit, Leon' *The Encyclopaedia of the Social Sciences* vol. 5 p. 272.
[139] See the works of Nicolas Politis and George Scelle in Europe, and in Latin America see *infra* Chapter 3.
[140] *Supra*, fn. 92.
[141] Fenwick, *International Law*, p 64.

Diverging in an interesting way from all viewpoints mentioned thus far is that of the Greek publicist, JEAN SPIROPOULOS (1896–   ), who observes that conflicting doctrines of international law are equally sound in that the experimenter is justified in choosing his own hypothesis and in delimiting his field as he may see fit [142]. The only really sound way to determine the matter, he says, is to consult the "dominant opinion" [143], meaning that the essence of international law is to be sought in human attitudes regarding it rather than in the intrinsic merit of any doctrine or system *per se*.

One of the most interesting of recent theoretical and practical developments in international law is the tendency of the past half century to view the individual as being in some measure a subject of the law of nations. During most of the modern period it has been commonplace to assume that only states and, especially as seen by Catholic writers, also the Vatican, were entitled to such recognition. Consequently the newer tendency referred to did not appear to any appreciable degree in the theory of international law of the early part of modern times. The chronological plan of development followed here accounts for the absence of earlier mention of this matter. It is, however, one of the most important advances to have been made in the theory of international law in modern times; and the present study will be concerned to inquire as to the extent of its appearance among Latin-American writers.

It is of the highest significance that many recent thinkers in this field have arrived at the view that the individual is entitled to be regarded as a subject of international law. Krabbe and Duguit were especially emphatic in this respect, holding that the individual person is, in fact, the *only* subject of the law of nations [144]. Many dualist writers, *e.g.*, Fenwick, have not been slow to recognize that the individual enjoys a degree of international personality [145], but the strongest emphasis in this direction has come, on the whole, from the monists.

---

[142] Spiropoulos, *op. cit.*, pp. 17–20 *et passim*.

[143] *Ibid.*, pp. 21–24 *et passim*.

[144] Krabbe, *op. cit.*, pp. 240–245. Also Nussbaum, *op. cit.*, pp. 283–285. For a recent statement by Kelsen of a similar view see his *Principles of International Law* (New York, Rinehart & Co., 1952), pp. 96–100, 114–117 *et passim*.

[145] Fenwick, *op. cit.*, pp. 132–135.

Recent works of PHILIP JESSUP (1897–   ) and of HERSH
LAUTERPACHT (1897–   ) have lent further weight to this important development. Jessup emphasizes that international law
must be reorganized to apply to individuals directly and, in
addition, that solidarity must be achieved to the extent that
breaches of the law are considered as affronteries to all nations [146].
Lauterpacht, in a somewhat similar vein, has been concerned
in recent years with the international rights of man, and seems
to see the international personality and the more or less natural
rights of man progressively coming into their own on the international scene by means of changing usages and under the
auspices of the United Nations Organization and of the Council
of Europe [147].

The ultimate significance of this development is that, along
with becoming a subject of international law, the individual is
placed in a closer relationship with a political authority theoretically above the heretofore omnipotent state. In the long run
the probabilities are that the individual will be considered as
responsible in considerable measure to international authority,
and the state will lose a degree of its Hobbesian-Hegelian
characteristics.

It must be emphasized that, although this last statement is,
manifestly, speculation regarding the possible development of
a relatively new theory of international law, it is not, however,
without its documentation. Perhaps the most important official
development in this direction in recent years has been the war
crimes trials, especially the Nuremburg Trials in which individuals were held directly liable for the acts of a nation [148].
There are, however, other evidences, not the least of which has
been the adoption by the United Nations of the Universal
Declaration of Human Rights [149] which, though as yet of less
legal than moral significance, nevertheless partakes to a degree
of both of these elements and constitutes what may well be

---

[146] Philip C. Jessup, *A Modern Law of Nations* (New York, The Macmillan Company, 1948).

[147] H. Lauterpacht, *International Law and Human Rights*.

[148] 'International Military Tribunal (Nuremberg), Judgment and Sentences' *The
American Journal of International Law*, (January, 1947), pp. 172–333.

[149] On this whole subject see H. Lauterpacht, *International Law and Human
Rights*, pp. 394–434 *et passim*.

another step in the establishment of the international personality of the individual.

It should be apparent from the foregoing sketch of the theory
of international law that this thought has in reality been part
of the history of political thought in general. As such it is clear,
too, that this aspect of legal philosophy has been strongly influenced by the facts of international life. It is to be expected that
Latin-American writers, like others, have been influenced by
their time and place in the human drama [150]. But it is true
also that the modern American culture is essentially a branch
of European culture. The influence of Europe's publicists on
Latin-American writers has been enormous; at the same time
particularist trends are much in evidence. It is, then, against
this whole background of legal thought in the Western World,
as well as against the background of the American scene as
such, that the following chapters must be viewed.

---

[150] William Rex Crawford, *A Century of Latin-American Thought* (Cambridge,
Harvard University Press, 1944), pp. 4-5.

CHAPTER II

THE LATIN AMERICAN WRITERS OF THE NINETEENTH CENTURY

Introduction

The previous chapter has shown that while the dominant trend throughout the nineteenth century was an inclination toward positivism, a great number of the publicists who participated in this trend at least paid their respects to the naturalistic tradition [1]. If this was generally true throughout the rest of the western world, it was almost wholly true in Latin America; *i.e.*, among those thinkers and writers who tended toward positivism in Latin America virtually all were disposed to at least acknowledge the existence of naturalistic forces as having legal implications.

In this sense, then, all these Latin American thinkers on international law are eclectics. The question is to determine whether their eclecticism is predominantly oriented toward naturalism or toward positivism, or, whether the classfication of *eclectic* must be left to stand unmodified.

An attempt will also be made to determine what inclination, if any, may be detected of a movement toward including more than states as subjects or persons of international law. This inquiry is especially directed toward the end of determining whether individual persons were thought to be justified in claiming international personality. With this object in view each publicist's definition of international law will be analyzed, together with other materials that may seem pertinent.

In this analysis it must be realized that when two writers

---

[1] *Supra*, Chapter I, see, *e.g.*, the remarks regarding Phillimore, Wheaton, and Fiore.

refer to natural law they may have in mind two somewhat
different phenomena. Furthermore, it is to be understood that
in attempting to evaluate divergent ideas of natural law, and
to weigh them in the light of what each writer means, or seems
to mean, by this term, and then also to try to judge how intensely
he believes in the conception, this altogether does not partake
of mathematical accuracy. The conclusions which are suggested
must be viewed in the light of the unavoidable subjectivity
which permeates the totality of the concepts appraised.

In addition to a survey of the views of these writers on the
extent to which naturalism may be considered an element in
the foundation of international law, and also their views regarding the international personality of the individual, the
writings of Juan Bautista Alberdi will be separately analyzed
in regard to their implications for international law. These
works of Alberdi will be taken up in a special section of the
chapter because it is felt that they do not readily fall into any
of the other sections, and can, therefore, best be treated as
a unique tradition. Next, a statement will be made regarding
certain titles which deserve to be cited in this work, but which,
for one reason or another, do not merit more than cursory
mention. Finally, a number of conclusions will be drawn.

A. THE POSITIVISTS

The first publicist of a systematic work in the field of international
law in Latin America was the versatile Venezuelan born ANDRES
BELLO (1781–1865). After many years abroad in the diplomatic
employ of Colombia and Chile, he returned to the latter nation
in 1829. In 1832 the first edition of his book, *Principios de
derecho de jentes,* was concluded, and it appeared the following
year [2]. It was written because there were apparently available
no teachable treatises of a satisfactory character. This work
was republished with some changes in 1844, and in 1864 it
appeared in a third edition under the slightly changed title of
Principios de derecho internacional, following a terminology which

---

[2] Andres Bello, 'Principios de derecho internacional' *Obras completas de Don
Andres Bello* Vol. X (Santiago de Chile, Impreso por Pedro G. Ramirez, 1885),
p. XIV.

Bello thought more idiomatic [3]. This is the edition reprinted in the *Obras completas* and the one used in this study.

The work follows generally the plan of Vattel [4], but a great emphasis has been placed on positivism. It has been highly influential in Latin America, as any survey of the works of Latin American publicists will indicate. It is apparent from the deference shown them by other writers that Bello along with Calvo were most probably the two best known writers of their region during the last century, and it may be noted that the American, Henry Wheaton, held the former in the highest esteem [5].

At numerous points Bello shows the naturalistic elements of his philosophy. He observes, for example, that "Since the nations are not subservient to one another, the laws or rules to which their reciprocal conduct must be subjected, can only be dictated to them by reason ... [6]." This reason, taking into consideration experience and the common well-being, is, in his view, "... deduced for them from the chain of causes and effects which we perceive in the physical and moral order of the universe [7]." He goes on to suggest that the Deity has established the causes and effects and is therefore in reality the true author of these laws. "International law, or the [law] of nations", he continues,

is nothing else, then, than the natural [law], which applied to the nations, considers the human race, spread over the face of the earth, as a great society of which each one of them is a member, and in which the ones in respect to the others have the same primordial duties as [have] individuals of the human species among themselves.

We ought, then, to look at them as so many moral persons [8].

Bello has a good deal to say about natural law in which he apparently believes implicity. He follows Vattel in breaking international law down into internal and external components, which in essence mean natural and positive or unenforceable and enforceable components, respectively.

---

[3] *Ibid.*, p. XV.
[4] *Ibid.*, p. XIV.
[5] *Ibid.*, p. XVI.
[6] *Ibid.*, p. 11.
[7] *Loc. cit.*
[8] *Ibid.*, p. 12.

The law of nations, or the collection of laws or international rules, is called *internal*, whenever it looks only to the conscience, and determines what is ordered, permitted or prohibited; and *external*, when it determines the obligations whose completion can be exacted by force [9].

Bello's philosophy is not always easy to understand, but at one point he makes a sufficiently clear statement of the Grotian position. While this is somewhat contradicted elsewhere, as will be seen later in this study, the Grotian point of view appears in the following remark:

That which does not have any other basis than reason or natural equity is called the *natural, universal common*, [and/or] *primitive* law of nations, and that which the express or tacit conventions have formed and whose sole force is derived indirectly from reason, which prescribes to the nations, as a rule of supreme importance, the inviolability of pacts [is called the] voluntary, special, conventional, positive [and/or] secondary [law of nations] [10].

Following the explanations which have just been outlined, Bello emphasizes that it is sometimes difficult to determine what natural law is and that specific laws are often needed [11]. "It is also necessary to confess", he says,

that from state to state the difference between external natural law and customary law is of pure theory. The truth is that there are a certain number of moral axioms which no one disputes in the abstract; but their application in particular cases occasions doubts and controversies at each step. Thus we see that the so-called natural law is variable and fluctuating, not only from century to century, but from nation to nation; and that a constant rule, though it appear reasonable and equitable, and though it be illuminated (*i.e.*, supported) [by] the demonstrations of the writers who defend it, does not begin to be rigorously observed, save when custom has sanctioned it... [12].

An illuminating remark is found in the prologue to the 1844 edition in which an explanation of the work appears. "I am convinced", he says,

that in the practical applications of this science the theoretical

---

[9] *Ibid.*, p. 16.
[10] *Ibid.*, p. 17. It should be pointed out that Bello considers customs as being tacit conventions.
[11] *Ibid.*, p. 18.
[12] *Ibid.*, p. 19.

deductions are worth much less than the positive rules, sanctioned by the conduct of civilized peoples and of powerful governments, and above all by the decisions of the tribunals which judge under the law of nations; and this conviction which served as a guide to me in the previous edition, has suggested almost all the enlargements, illustrations and notes with which I have wished to better the present [work] [13].

Bello defines international law as "... the collection of laws or general rules of conduct which the nations or states must (*deben*) observe among themselves for their security and common well-being [14]." There is not in this definition, nor elsewhere, as far as has been ascertained by the present writer, any suggestion or other indication that some entity other than the conventional parties might be considered persons or subjects of international law.

The most logical conclusion to be drawn is that Andres Bello's practical orientation is clearly toward positivism, but that naturalist considerations are not abandoned; also that Bello's conception of the subjects or persons of international law is traditional.

The Paraguayan, D. RAMON FERREIRA, wrote his *Lecciones de derecho internacional* originally as a text for students while he was a professor at the Colejio de Tacna in Peru. At the time the book was published in 1861 he was the attorney general (*fiscal*) of the state supreme court.

Ferreira suggests initially that international law is a natural law phenomenon. He defines it as "... that which considers the external relations of the nations with each other ...", and is persuaded that "... it conforms to the general interest and to the principles of natural law [15]." Its authority, he thinks, is derived from the natural law [16].

At a later point he makes the observation that international law can be divided into natural and positive sections. The former "... is founded only in reason and in the universal principles of natural justice ... [17]." The latter is "... instituted by the

---

[13] *Ibid.*, p. 6.
[14] *Ibid.*, p. 11.
[15] D. Ramon Ferreira, *Lecciones de derecho internacional* (Paraná, Imprenta nacional, 1861), p. 1.
[16] *Loc. cit.*
[17] *Ibid.*, p. 2.

express or tacit consent of nations founded in pact or custom ... [18]." The latter, according to Ferreira, is binding only on those who are committed by pact or custom to uphold them; the former are binding on all without reference to either consent or custom, and their authority is *"ex-vigore legis naturalis"* [19]. The positive law is perfect and external, *i.e.*, its obligation is complete and "always exercises external coaction," whereas the natural law, being not always perfect, raises the question as to when it is internal and hence only subject to the sanction of conscience, and when it is external or binding in the legal, as contrasted with the moral, sense [20]. Ferreira's explanation of this situation is a most interesting instance of what seems to this writer to be, for all practical purposes, a positivist postion. "The difficult question", he says,

which is presented is to determine in practice the cases in which the universal law is perfect or external and those in which it is obligatory only in conscience; because although the natural law rests on principles of morality which nobody doubts, when one treats of its application and, much more, [when] mediating conflicting interests, [then] doubts and different interpretations always result, and with the exception of very clear cases, it only comes to be recognized as perfect law when it is sanctioned by convention or custom [21].

The three "general rules and sources" of international law which Ferreira mentions are:

1. the uniform opinion of the most distinguished authors, ...
2. The decisions of the admiralty courts, and tribunals of international justice; and the regulations and ordinances given by the most advanced powers for the direction of their courts, and for the understanding among other nations of the principles of the universal law which they (*i.e.*, the advanced powers) recognize.
3. When in all the conventions or most of them (*o con generalidad*), some principle of natural law accepted as unquestionable is adopted (*se ve adoptado*) by the nations [22].

It seems that the essence of these remarks is a virtually complete

---

[18] *Loc. cit.*
[19] *Ibid.*, pp. 2–3.
[20] *Ibid.*, p. 3.
[21] *Loc. cit.*
[22] *Ibid.*, pp. 3–4.

capitulation to positivism. Ferreira's definition of international law together with his further commentary indicate no noticeable deviation from traditional views regarding the persons or subjects of international law.

Undoubtedly the best known of nineteenth century Latin American writers in the area of international law was the Argentine, CARLOS CALVO (1824–93). His reputation rested on a vast diplomatic experience as well as upon the written work which is reviewed here. This went through five editions from the first two-volume Spanish edition of 1868 to the six-volume French edition of 1896. The five-volume fourth edition of 1887 has been used in the present study.

Calvo covers a wealth of material, and both his method and his confessed philosophy are of a positivist character. In regard to the former it may be observed that he mentions the classification of international law as commonly accepted by seventeenth and eighteenth century jurists, systematically and briefly explaining each of the categories of divine law, positive law, conventional law, and customary law, together with a short section dealing with still other classifications made by some writers [23]. He then goes on to say that the classifications which the early publicists saw fit to establish have lost much of their significance since they reflect excessively subtle distinctions which have little or no relation to the realities of international life. It is, nevertheless, a matter which he feels bound to discuss out of deference to customary practice [24].

States are much like the medieval feudal barons who recognized no tribunals over them, suggests Calvo, and then asks how one would apply the principles of justice to their inter-relations. His answer is characteristically positivist. A short paragraph or two is devoted to each of sixteen outstanding writers from Gentili to Mancini in which the system of each of these men is outlined [25]. This is followed with a statement of Calvo's own theory such as confirms the method and practices used throughout his work. "For our part", he says,

---

[23] Charles Calvo, *Le droit international théorique et pratique*, Tome I (Paris, Guillaumin et Cie., 1887), pp. 142–144.

[24] *Ibid.*, pp. 144–145.

[25] *Ibid.*, pp. 145–154.

we recognize that the general idea of justice can modify the relations of states to their well-being and common profit; nevertheless in the course of our work we shall attach preference to principles defined by treaties, to rules which are deduced naturally and logically from particular conventions or from diverse instances resolved in practice, [and] finally to sanctioned jurisprudence [26].

At another point he emphasizes that treaties constitute the principal source of international law [27].

By way of definition this author maintains simply that the "... law of nations, or international law [is] the aggregate of rules of conduct observed by the several nations in their relations among themselves ... [28]."

Thus the evidence would seem unequivocally to indicate that Calvo is as nearly a complete positivist as one could expect to find in the nineteenth century. Unlike his predecessor, Bello, he shows only the most perfunctory respect for the natural law tradition. Also, his appraisal of the persons of international law results in much the same traditional position assumed by Bello.

RAFAEL FERNANDO SEIJAS (1822–1901 supposed) was, like Andres Bello, Venezuelan born. He wrote several works in the areas of international law, diplomatic affairs, and politics, of which his six-volume work on public and private Hispanic-American international law, published in 1884, is the source of interest here.

This interesting work, which resembles John Bassett Moore's *Digest of International Law* [29] perhaps more than any other American work, is truly a monument to positivism. He concentrates largely on the practices of states and the opinions of writers and of courts.

This author observes that his object is to produce a work which will bring together the completed international law actions of his land, and if possible of all Latin America, thus to provide a guide or consultative source for dealing with European and other nations [30]. He is, however, interested in seeing a confeder-

[26] *Ibid.*, p. 154.
[27] *Ibid.*, pp. 159–160.
[28] *Ibid.*, p. 139.
[29] *Supra*, Chapter I, fn. 101.
[30] Rafael Fernando Seijas, *El derecho internacional hispano americano* Vol. I (Caracas, Imprenta de 'El Monitor', 1884), p. 1.

ation along the lines of the United States covering Latin America — especially a reconstituted greater Columbia [31]. To these ends he aims to "codify the Hispanic-American international legislation [32]."

Seijas is not much given to theorizing; he seems not even to define international law. He deals, however, specifically with the sources of international law. The rather lengthy statement on this point appears in the midst of his treatment of consular affairs, yet it bears on the entire work and is quite consistent with the remainder of his study. He is not satisfied with the Grotian division of international law into *necessary* and *voluntary* law, nor does he find the terminology often used to avoid the Grotian dichotomy more appropriate to his science [33]. He proceeds to define his own terms. "Ahead of everything else", says Seijas,

I recognize the *positive public law*: that is to say, the aggregate of laws, edicts, and judgments, proclaimed under the regular authority of each country or by some temporary authority, establishing rules for reciprocal relations (*inteligencia*) with foreign peoples. Such are the *decisions of the Supreme Court* of justice of the *United States*, the *decisions* of *Parliament*, of the *Crown* or of the *Admiralty* in England, the *ordinances* of the *kings* or of the *assemblies* of *France etc.* etc.
   In second place I put *conventional law proper*: [*i.e.*, the rules embodied] in treaties, conventions, and other stipulations of the nation itself with foreign [states]; namely those which become laws, not by mere use of the country itself, but *by convention*.
   Part of this conventional law proper is called customary, when it is founded on practices [in which the nation itself participates].
   In third place [is] *foreign conventional law*, or the body of principles and practices most generally established and accepted by other civilized people of the world, whether in their treaties and conventions [or] whether in their [customary] acts; those which become rules [that], if not obligatory, [are] at least lawful, in the absence of positive *law* and of *coventional law proper*.
   Regarding this *foreign conventional law* it seems to me that it is part of what is called *customary law*, when it is maintained

---

[31] *Ibid.*, p. XVI.
[32] *Ibid.*, p. VII.
[33] *Ibid.*, p. 419.

not by repetition of our own, but by repetition of foreign practices.

In fourth place it seems to me one ought to put the *natural, common, or primitive public law*; or, in other words, that which applies the principles of the *natural law* to the relations of peoples and of governments among themselves; because those principles, although they have been the origin of all laws, and treaties, and practices, and [indeed of all] existing things, cannot by themselves rule except in so far as they are not opposed to *positive law*, to *conventional law proper*, or to *foreign conventional law*.

In fifth place, it seems to me, is *voluntary law*, that is to say, the decisions which, with relation to the mere convenience of each people, would be sustained in the exercise of a legitimate freedom, or inherent right, to select without prejudice to the intangible principles of justice the most adequate or honest interests; and this *voluntary public law*, I think, is what the scientific authorities mean whenever they refer to the convenience of the human race, inseparable from justice [34].

This statement, although at times a bit abstruse, reveals on the whole with sufficient force and clarity the philosophical orientation of the author. There can be virtually no doubt that Seijas is, like Calvo, as complete a positivist as the nineteenth century could be expected to produce.

From the material available to this writer no definite statement can be made regarding Seijas' views on the subjects or persons of international law. However, from the general flavor of the writings, one would be inclined to assume his position to be essentially traditional.

One of the very few early systematic Mexican works on international law is that of JOSÉ H. RAMIREZ. It was published in 1870 for the use of the public authorities, for foreigners, and for the use of students [35].

Although he speaks of the usual two parts of international law, *i.e.*, natural and positive law, he does not think of the former as being derived from a supposed natural state which, according to a then prevailing view, existed prior to the social state. On the contrary, he derives it from " . . . the situation of the different associations of men which we call nations . . . [36]."

---

[34] *Ibid.*, pp. 419–420.

[35] José H. Ramirez, *Codigo de los extranjeros; introduccion al estudio del derecho internacional desde los tiempos antiguos hasta nuestros dias* (Mexico, Imprenta de I. Escalante y ca., 1870), p. VI.

[36] *Ibid.*, p. 5.

Ramirez makes it fairly clear that his method has been to search the codes of Mexico and of other nations, and to utilize those rules of international law which are universally recognized [37]. He has little or nothing to do with naturalism. "... it is necessary", he observes,

to abstract and exclude from this study, in so far as possible, all those principles which can be called ethics or morality of nations, in order to consider international law as the collection of rules which regulate or ought to (*deben de*) regulate the relations among the various states or independent nations. Our study is directed toward the investigation of the legal or juridical relations which exist among the various societies or aggregates of men, which, occupying a part of the surface of the globe, are called nations. We shall occupy ourselves only with those laws and obligations that are properly so-called in that they are susceptible of coaction, either by reason of the justice which surrounds them, or, and more principally, by the convenience which results to all the rest of the nations from sustaining their observance [38].

The positive law in his view is derived from conventions, usages, and customs [39].

There would seem to be relatively little doubt as to the fundamental orientation of this publicist. While he does not completely abandon the natural law, he is basically concerned with the more positivist elements. Furthermore, it seems apparent that his conceptions of the persons or subjects of international law is traditional.

In addition to the nineteenth century writers of a positivistic orientation who have just been reviewed, there are two authors whose works have been thought to be borderline, but sufficiently within the orbit of the scheme of this work to merit a few remarks.

The first of these is the little book of ANGEL TREMOSA Y NADAL, (1856–99), published in Habana in 1896. It will be recalled that Cuba was then a Spanish colony, which fact explains that Tremosa y Nadal, though at the time in Latin America, was a First Lieutenant in the Spanish army. The book, approved by the Spanish crown, had been written for the author's companions in arms.

---

[37] *Ibid.*, pp. VI-VIII.
[38] *Ibid.*, pp. 4–5.
[39] *Ibid.*, p. 6.

International law is defined by Tremosa y Nadal as "... the aggregate of laws or general rules of conduct which the nations must (*deben*) observe among themselves, whether it be in peace or in war [40]."

It is to his section on the sources of international law that one must turn for anything approximating a clear statement of his views regarding naturalism or positivism. Treaties and custom are, he says, the chief sources of international law. In some cases he views scientific law, *i.e.*, the writings of the publicists, and jurisprudence, *i.e.*, the doctrines of the courts, as proper sources also [41]. He speaks, however, of natural law as well as of positivistic sources, at one point observing that "War is from the natural law ... [42]." Elsewhere he notes that international law is to be considered from three viewpoints: 1. the philosophical, which he seems to think of as explaining "... the conditions of coexistence and social intercourse of peoples ...;" 2. the historical or positive, which embraces (*a*) philosophical science (probably referring to the writings of the publicists), (*b*) usages and customs, and (*c*) conventions; and 3. the political, which he apparently does not explain [43].

The second of the two borderline works is a small book published in 1897 in Santiago de Chile. This was a translation of a work by G. BOURDON-VIANE, a French academician, whose writings have embraced both public and private international law.

Bourdon-Viane suggests that international law is obligatory, but that it has only the sanction of the moral law. War is merely "... the right (*razon*) of the strongest," and hence, apparently, not a valid sanction [44]. He seems to put international law in somewhat the same category as constitutional law, and then points out that the force of public opinion, while not great, is nevertheless taken into consideration by governments [45].

As to sources, he mentions treaties, compilations of treaties,

---

[40] Angel Tremosa y Nadal, *Nociones de derecho internacional* (Habana, 'La Australia', 1896), p. 11.

[41] *Ibid.*, p. 14.

[42] *Ibid.*, p. 60.

[43] *Ibid.*, p. 12.

[44] G. Bourdon-Viane, *Compendio de derecho internacional publico* (Santiago de Chile, Imp. Mejia, 1897), pp. 9–10.

[45] *Ibid.*, p. 10.

national laws, customary laws, and works of the publicists [46].

In defining international law, he says that:

It is the aggregate of rules regarding the relations of one state with another, or with the subjects of another state, or, even, with its own subjects [who are] inhabitants of another state [47].

It may be concluded that in both of these cases the writings tend to emphasize the positive aspects, and also that the conception of Tremosa y Nadal regarding the persons or subjects of international law is traditional. What Bourdon-Viane has in mind as to this last mentioned matter is not clear from the available evidence. However, in view of his interest in private as well as in public international law, it may be conjectured that his thought on this point was essentially traditional; but it must be emphasized again that this conclusion is at best a surmise.

B. THE ECLECTICS

The little volume, published in 1867, by ANTONIO DE VASCON-CELLOS MENZES DE DRUMMOND (1819–76) was written primarily for the use of students [48]. This Brazilian writer, presumably a follower of Pedro da Autram e Alburquerque Matta [49], wrote also on the subject of diplomacy.

This author makes the usual division of international law into natural and positive segments. The former, in his view, serves several purposes among which are the maintenance of the dictates of justice, guaranteeing reciprocal duties, serving as a complement to (or for the interpreting of) imperfect treaties, and constituting the theory of the positive law of nations. Positive law, on the other hand, embraces principles which have been assented to by the nation, national jurisprudence for the maintenance of international relations, treaties, usages, and customs [50].

Observing that the foundation of the natural law branch of

[46] *Ibid.*, pp. 11–16.

[47] *Ibid.*, p. 9.

[48] Antonio Vasconcellos Menzes de Drummond, *Prelecções de direito internacional* (Pernambuco, Tipographia do correio do Recife, 1867), p. 6.

[49] *Infra*, p. 74.

[50] Vasconcellos, *op. cit.*, p. 10.

international law is in "... the nature itself of the relations which exist among nations ... [51]", he defines international law as "... the collection of individual and reciprocal laws among the nations themselves, or on the other hand — [as drawn] from the judgments founded in justice, or adduced from the mutual relations and express conventions among them [52]." It may be added that he uses the terms state and nation synonomously [53].

There is really very little from which to judge the degree of positivism followed by this author. His remark that the natural law serves, among other things, as a theory of the positive law [54], may be an indication of one of several points of view. It may, for example, mean that he accepts the basic norm *pacta sunt servanda* seen as grounded in the natural law. On the other hand, one can just as reasonably conclude from his view as set forth that the natural law is founded in "... the nature itself of the relations which exist among nations ... [55]", that positive rules are geared to this international relationship and hence derive their "theory" from the natural law which in itself is a product of the same international relationship.

Whether either of these views is sound is largely a matter of conjecture, and in view of the lack of information necessary to draw a conclusion, and due to the ambiguousness of some of the material which is at hand, Vasconcellos' view must be left, more or less by default, in the eclectic category. As to the persons or subjects of international law, he seems to be entirely traditional.

The Colombian publicist, MANUEL MARÍA MADIEDO (1815–88), whose writings include philosophy, politics, poetry, and a wide variety of interests, wrote, in 1874, the rather philosophical work on international law which is surveyed here.

Madiedo makes a distinction between the law of nations or peoples (*derecho de jentes* or *jus gentium*) and international law (*derecho internacional* or *derecho entre naciones*). The former designates "... the application of universal morality to the relations of all the *peoples* of the earth ... [56]." Furthermore, it is the

---

[51] *Ibid.*, p. 9.
[52] *Loc. cit.*
[53] *Ibid.*, fn. p. 12.
[54] *Ibid.*, p. 10.
[55] *Supra*, fn. 51.
[56] Manuel María Madiedo, *Tratado de derecho de jentes, internacional, diplomatico i consular* (Bogotá, Tipografia de Nicolas Ponton i compañia, 1874), p. 3.

"... science of good and evil and the basis of all positive law [57]."

International law, on the other hand,
... is the aggregate of principles, rules, customs and practices sanctioned by nations properly so-called (*propiamente dichas*) by virtue of treaties, conventions, practices, and customs [58].

Although Madiedo sets up a legal hierarchy which on the surface appears to be positivistically inclined, his basic legal views, on closer analysis, seem to have a good deal of naturalism about them. When a problem of international law arises, it is advised that sources be consulted in the following order:

1. The written law: treaties, conventions, etc.
2. Mutual or universal custom, verified by recognized practices.
3. Analogy of the case at hand (*caso ocurrente*) with others forseen in treaties, conventions or customs of the nations which are debating any question whatsoever.
4. The fundamental principles of international law.
5. The law of nations [or peoples] (*derecho de jentes*), such as we have defined it [59].

In spite of this positivism, however, a naturalistic flavor often predominates. At one point it is observed that the law of nations or peoples (*derecho de jentes*) is primary and that it supplies the scientific element in the regulation of international affairs; it is, in his view, the original moral law. It is said further that positive written law and positive customary law, "... when they do not part ways with justice are nothing but applications of the universal moral law to the individual exigencies of nations ... [60]." At still another point it is made abundantly clear how fundamental this author considers the naturalistic element to be:

It is clear, then, that the true sources and the true authority of international law, are [to be found] not in the authors, nor in the institutions, nor in international practices, *in general*, but in the scientific principles of such interesting material; which are nothing other than those which are deduced from the great eternal moral law [directed] toward the conditions of existence of the nature of men. That is not to say that the opinions

---

[57] *Loc. cit.*
[58] *Ibid.*, p. 4.
[59] *Ibid.*, pp. 9–10.
[60] *Ibid.*, p. 25.

of the publicists of public law are not consulted concerning the true doctrines and practices authorized by the nations. What we have wished is not to exclude these, but to assign them their true category [61].

At a later point Madiedo observes that international law in the last analysis is a deduction from the law of peoples (*derecho de jentes*) [62].

The apparent contradiction tends to leave one in a quandary as to how this publicist should be classified. Perhaps, in view of the apparent ambiguity, it is best to consider him an eclectic. It is safe to conclude that as far as his views of the persons or subjects of international law are concerned, he is essentially traditional.

MANUEL ATANASIO FUENTES (1820–87), a Peruvian, wrote in 1876 an "Encyclopedia of Law" in which all of the more important branches of law were treated. The third volume contains several elements of an international concern, such as international law, diplomatic law, private international law, several aspects of Roman law, and canon law. Only the section dealing with international law is noted here.

Fuentes considers only states as subjects of international law, and it is with these entities that he concerns himself [63]. International law is said to be "... the aggregate of rules which determine the reciprocal rights and duties of Nations ...[64]." This applies both in time of peace and of war.

Regarding the foundation of international law, he makes the Pufendorfian remark that international law must consist of the natural laws and nothing else. This follows from the status of nations as moral persons living in a state of nature. "Among them there are no tribunals, nor common superior; only justice imposes its laws on them [65]."

In spite of this statement, Fuentes acknowledges the usual dichotomy of natural and positive segments of international law, as deriving respectively from reason alone and from express

---

[61] *Ibid.*, p. 30.
[62] *Ibid.*, p. 31.
[63] Manuel A. Fuentes, 'Derecho internacional' *Curso de encyclopedia del derecho.* Tomo III (Lima, Imprenta del estado, 1876), pp. 4–12 *et passim*.
[64] *Ibid.*, p. 1.
[65] *Ibid.*, p. 2.

or tacit agreements. The force of the latter, however, is seen to stem indirectly from reason [66].

As to sources of international law, seven are mentioned in the following order:

1. The teachings of the publicists which show the rules of justice as applicable to the international community and the variations of these which usage and general consent allow;

2. treaties;

3. war-time national laws for regulating prize cases;

4. decisions of international courts;

5. the confidential opinions of legists to their governments in regard to disputed questions;

6. proclamations, manifestos and diplomatic correspondence; and

7. "The doctrine compiled in the ancient writings and the great collections of the Roman jurisconsults [67]."

It is evident that Fuentes' work contains elements of both naturalism and positivism. The former occupy, certainly, a prominent enough place to make it appropriate to designate him as an eclectic if not, indeed, to classify him as a naturalist. His ideas on the subjects or persons of international law are traditional.

FEDERICO DIEZ DE MEDINA (1839–1904), a Bolivian law professor at the University of La Paz and a writer in the areas of constitutional and international law, produced in the latter field in 1883 an interesting little text for class use.

The composition of international law having been outlined, the following summary indicates the eclectic flavor of this work:

In summary, this law [when] well contemplated is composed:
1. of incontrovertible truths, fundamental or invariable maxims which cannot be designated properly except with the name of principles; and
2. of certain variable obligations or regulations only created by customs or agreements, and which can be called simply rules of conduct [68].

There appears no indication that Diez de Medina wanted to

---

[66] *Loc. cit.*

[67] *Ibid.*, pp. 3–4.

[68] Federico Diez de Medina, *Nociones de derecho internacional* (Paris, Imprenta de Julio Le Clere, 1883), p. 9.

convey the positivistic impression of the superiority of customs and treaties. His definition of international law together with supplementary remarks bear this out.

International law is the aggregate of principles and customary rules of conduct, which the states must (*deben*) observe in their mutual relations.

Its precepts are deduced as much from the recognized prescriptions of reason and justice as from the practices and usages generally admitted by the civilized nations; its aggregate includes the successive modifications constantly introduced by the agreement of peoples and by the progress of the ideas of justice [69].

At another point this author, in speaking of the sources, first lists treaties which, he observes, draw their binding force from the natural law. Secondly he mentions custom. Thirdly, when neither treaties nor pertinent customary usages are at hand, the sources of natural law as interpreted by human reason are to be called upon [70]. Writers, in his view, are an important aid in finding and applying these three sources. Also marine ordinances and international court decisions, constitute application of these sources since they are regarded as being, in reality, derived from international law rather than as sources in themselves [71].

In speaking of this same matter, however, the author elsewhere makes this interesting distinction:

It must be noted that in case these sources are taken [*i.e.*, understood], as Phillimore, Hallek and other writers do, *theoretically*, or in the sense of their being the fundamentals or constitutive elements of the international science, it will be necessary to invert the order of their enumeration, locating in the first place the natural or divine law, from which are deduced the principles of justice and the rules to which states must subject themselves in their mutual relations [72].

Diez cites Heffter to the effect that in order to be valid a treaty must have a lawful motive, suggesting that treaties of an unlawful character would include those "... contrary to the moral order of things or to the general rights of humanity ...." Ex-

---

[69] *Ibid.*, pp. 1–2.
[70] *Ibid.*, p. 25.
[71] *Ibid.*, p. 26.
[72] *Loc. cit.*

amples given are such as the introduction of slavery or the complete abolition of commerce [73].

These remarks must, however, be weighed against the following statement regarding the procedure which ought to be followed in practical cases. "... it is indubitable", says Diez de Medina in summing up his essay on the subject,

that in the solution of practical cases, the positive law must (*deben*) prevail always when its prescriptions in a true and incontestable form exist, and the *rational* element, when there is vagueness, *lacuna*, or absolute lack of the first [74].

It is difficult, indeed, to determine any marked preference in Diez de Medina's view. He must be classed, therefore, in the eclectic group without making any attempt to specify more definitely his positivist or naturalist inclinations. As to his conceptions of the subjects or persons of international law, it would seem that his views are basically traditional.

One of the better known writers in Latin America was the Argentine, AMANCIO ALCORTA (1842–1902), who wrote rather widely on public and private international law, constitutional law, economics, and even education. The work which is to be surveyed here was published in 1887, and is apparently an abridged French version of an earlier and larger volume written in Spanish. Both of these works were designated as volume one of projected sets which seem never to have been completed.

Alcorta defines international law as

... the mass of rules designed (*destinées*) to regulate the relations of states and to determine the laws and usages applicable to the relations of private law which is born under the authority (*empire*) of the laws or usages of different states [75].

A clear point is made of the relationship between law (*loi*) and what is perhaps best translated here as "right" in the sense of ideal law (*droit*). "The right exists without the law, and the law is not always the perfect manifestation of the right, nor its only source [76]." The right, he feels, can and has existed without

---

[73] *Ibid.*, p. 101.
[74] *Ibid.*, pp. 26–27.
[75] Amancio Alcorta, *Cours de droit internacional public* (Paris, L. Larose et Forcel, 1887), pp. 33–34.
[76] *Ibid.*, p. 40.

law, but the reverse cannot happen because a society can exist without law, but not without the right. Both, however, stem from man; "the will of men" constitutes the law, while "... the essential precepts flowing from human nature constitute the right [77]." Law should emulate right, for "... the law takes its most perfect form when it succeeds in placing itself in accord with the precepts of the right [78]."

Speaking more specifically of international law, Alcorta suggests that the science thereof is to be observed from two viewpoints: from that of what ought to be, and from the viewpoint of what is. The former is universal, the latter is applicable only to those who have agreed to it [79].

As to the nature of the foundations, Alcorta makes the following remark:

... the basis (*fondement*) of international law is found in principles in the nature common to all men, and ... it is manifested progressively by the consent of the most civilized peoples. International law, said the English government to King Frederick II of Prussia, is founded on justice, equity and the nature of things and it is confirmed by a long usage [80].

As to whether Alcorta is more nearly a positivist, a naturalist or a true eclectic, one may turn to his own statement of faith. He describes eclecticism as being based on "... the principles of justice and the modifications introduced by custom, usage, conventions and treaties [81]", and later suggests that the eclectic school is the most nearly correct of the approaches to international law.

The eclectic school without doubt is that which most nearly approaches the truth, although the natural law, as much as or perhaps more than the positive law, cannot assume an immutable form in its applications, and one can only consider it as an aggregate of rules open to any and all modification. Nothing shows this better than the divergencies of opinions of those very ones who affirm its necessary character: in order to be convinced of this, it is enough to analyze the works of Wolf and of Vattel [82].

[77] *Loc. cit.*
[78] *Loc. cit.*
[79] *Ibid.*, p. 47.
[80] *Ibid.*, p. 107.
[81] *Ibid.*, p. 99.
[82] *Ibid.*, p. 102.

In the light of the above evidence, it is apparent that Alcorta is an eclectic, and that his conception of the persons or subjects of international law is traditional.

OSCAR RODRÍGUEZ SARÁCHAGA (1867–1936) was another Argentine whose writing on international law falls within the orbit of this chapter. He wrote also on the general subject of the administration of justice, but the interest here is in his book written in 1895 as a textbook for classroom use. It is little more than an elementary compilation of opinions, and apparently the author is much indebted to his compatriot, Amancio Alcorta.

After treating the various schools, he quotes Alcorta, seemingly with approbation, to the effect that the eclectic school most nearly approximates the truth [83].

He observes with Alcorta that since nations are merely groups of humans, one must seek the basis of international law in the same place as the basis of private law, *i.e.*, in the nature of man [84]. This view is well represented in the following quotation which Rodríguez Saráchaga takes from Alcorta:

The basis of international law, it has been said, is found in the nature common to all men, being manifested progressively by the consent of the most civilized peoples: it is based, then, on justice, equity, and the nature of things and is confirmed by a long usage [85].

Rodríguez Saráchaga holds, as regarding definition [86], and, in fact, in all important respects, to the same opinions held by Amancio Alcorta.

C. THE NATURALISTS

The work of JOSÉ MARÍA DE PANDO (1787–1840), first published in 1843 and later in 1852, may be considered as one of the most intriguing of the Latin American contributions to international law. The work, though widely known, is remarkable in that while there is much evidence of plagiarism, it does not seem to

---

[83] O. Rodríguez Saráchaga, *El derecho internacional público* (Buenos Aires, Impr. litografía y encuadernación de teodomiro real y prado, 1895), p. 19. See also *supra*, fn. 82.

[84] *Ibid.*, p. 19.

[85] *Loc. cit.*

[86] *Ibid.*, p. 3. See also *supra*, fn. 75.

bear the philosophical marks of the work copied, *i.e.*, while Bello gives a positivistic turn [87] to his eclecticism, Pando's work is of quite a naturalistic bent [88]. There has been no attempt here to determine the extent to which this questionable practice was indulged in, but suffice it to say that in some instances successive pages were lifted from Bello's work without appreciable acknowledgement being given [89], and incorporated into that of Pando. In some of these cases the only originality shown is an occasional change in punctuation or the slightly altered beginning or ending of a paragraph [90].

Pando was born in Lima, Peru, but was educated in Spain. He had diplomatic experience both under the Spanish and under the Peruvian governments and wrote on various subjects besides international law including politics, diplomacy, and morality [91].

Pando is often anything but clear, but he seems to recognize the usual dichotomy in international law: the necessary law which is impelling on the conscience only, and the voluntary law which depends upon consent, *i.e.*, conventions either tacit

---

[87] *Supra*, pp. 39–42.

[88] Andres Bello, 'Elementos de derecho internacional por José María de Pando' *Obras completas de Don Andres Bello*, Vol. X. p. 540. Bello suggests here that Pando has made a faithful translation of his ideas and phrases, but a little later (pp. 540–541) he speaks of Pando's philosophical notions as embodying too much Germanic metaphysics.

[89] José María de Pando, *Elementos del derecho internacional* (Madrid, Imprente de J. Martin Alegria, 1852), p. 48. Here he speaks of Bello's work as having great merit and as one to which he is deeply indebted. He also observes that only rarely has he seen fit to oppose Bello's views. Cf. Bello, 'Elementos de derecho internacional por José María de Pando.' p. 540. Bello does not speak harshly about the matter, saying he has "less reason to feel put out about it than to be grateful" as Pando has added something in the way of erudition and philosophical grace (*galas*). He does speak of Pando's work, however, as "... almost ... a new edition ..." of his own work.

[90] The following statements, the former of which is from Bello, *Principios de derecho internacional*, p. 17, and the latter from Pando, *op. cit.*, p. 9, point up this fact:

Se llama derecho de jentes *natural, universal, comun, primitivo, primario*, el que no tiene otro fundamento que la razon o la equidad natural, i *voluntario, especial, convencional, positivo, secundario*, el que han formado las convenciones expresas o tácitas, i cuya fuerza solo se deriva mediatamente de la razon, que prescribe a las naciones, como regla de importancia suprema, la inviolabilidad de los pactos.

Se llama derecho de gentes *natural—comun—universal—primitivo*—el que no tiene otro fundamento que la *razon* ó la *equidad natural*; y *arbitrario—especial —convencional—positivo*—el que formado las *convenciones*, expresas ó tácitas, y cuya fuerza solo se deriva mediatamente de la razon, que prescribe á las naciones como regla de importancia suprema, la inviolabilidad de los pactos.

[91] Bello, 'Elementos de derecho internacional por José María de Pando,' pp. 537–541.

or express [92]. This latter segment of international law, however, is also grounded on the natural law, for, in Pando's view, the inviolability of treaties has the injunction of natural law [93].

Pando is much concerned with sanctions, and sees religion as the chief of these in international law. The penalty is that which Divine Justice will see fit to inflict upon those who dare to transgress the natural law. Public opinion represents another sanction but in the international sphere it is of lesser importance [94].

Regarding the positivist writers he says:

Unfortunately, all the writers belonging to the school called *positivist*, have dedicated themselves (particularly the Germans) to treat exclusively of this conventional law, neglecting the natural [law] which ought to be its basis, its pure and salutary source. In the course of this treatment, we shall have many occasions to reproach them for this vicious fondness for signalling out the variable practices, at times contradictory, and repeatedly absurd or unjust, as true principles of a science sprung from eternal reason [95].

At another point he makes it quite clear that he considers conventional law as only a more formalized version of natural law. "The law introduced by pacts and customs," he says,

is to primitive [*i.e.*, natural] international law — what the civil code of each people is to the precepts and prohibitions of the natural law. It then makes specific and regularizes what was vague in the primitive law, and [what] needed fixed rules [96].

There is, however, another side to Pando. It is here that he shows some inclination toward positivism. In explaining why he wrote his book, he suggests that Spanish translations of foreign works (the only texts available, according to him) tend to be too abstract and do not give enough attention to the positive laws [97].

At another point Pando asks, in effect, what is to be done about the unfortunate lack of a code of natural and customary international law. He answers by suggesting recourse to the

---

[92] Pando, *op. cit.*, pp. 8–9.
[93] *Ibid.*, p. 9.
[94] *Ibid.*, pp. 2–3.
[95] *Ibid.*, pp. 9–10. This does not seem to be a plagiarized passage.
[96] *Ibid.*, p. 11. This is virtually a direct steal from Bello, *Principios de derecho internacional*, p. 18.
[97] Pando, *op., cit.* p. VII.

"eternal maxims of morality" and to the works of "accredited writers of international jurisprudence [98]."

He defines international law in the following terms:

The independent states considered in their mutual relations as moral persons are called peoples (*gentes*) or free nations. The aggregate of their reciprocal and perfect rights [and] of the law of the states among themselves forms the commonly so-called law of nations (*derecho de gentes*) or, according to the modern expression, international law. This is nothing else, according to the common understanding, than the collection of those laws or general rules of conduct which the nations *must* (*deben*) use reciprocally in order to guarantee their security and common well-being. This is what ordinarily is understood as natural law, applied whenever possible (*en lo posible*) to the nations, considering the human race spread over the face of the earth as a great society, of which each state is a member, and in which each and all with respect to each other have the same rights and the same duties which individuals of the human species have among themselves [99].

It may be concluded, then, that Pando is much less clear than Bello, because, in his plagiarism he is somewhat selective and often omits selections in which Bello clarifies his generalizations [100]. Whereas Bello seems clear, consistent, and logical in his development, Pando impresses one as being somewhat more vague, as having less command of his subject, and as being less sure of his own theoretical and practical convictions. The judgment that Pando is more naturalistically inclined is drawn from the seemingly less sincere and less strong remarks about the use of positivism in international law, and from the general flavor of the work as a whole. This conclusion should be viewed, however, in the light of the highly subjective considerations which are involved.

It may be safely concluded also that Pando's view of the persons or subjects of international law is traditional.

---

[98] *Ibid.*, p. 15.

[99] *Ibid.*, p. 1. Cf., Bello, *Principios de derecho internacional*, pp. 11-12. Also *supra* fn. 8.

[100] It may be conjectured that this could have been due in part to the fact that Pando's manuscript was lost for a time before it was published. It may also be partly due to the fact that Pando's work would have been published in 1838 if it had not been lost, and that he must have used the first edition of Bello's work which may have differed to a degree from the edition used in this survey. However, *cf.*, *supra*, fn. 88.

Of all the naturalistically inclined writers who are reviewed in this study, one of the most emphatic in his position is the Uruguayan, GREGORIO PEREZ GOMAR (1834–85). He has written, in addition to this study of international law, works in the field of natural law and also regarding the early explorer, Americus Vespucius. It is pertinent to note that the work reviewed here, which was published in 1864, contains an introduction dealing with natural law, and it may be categorically stated that the author's entire orientation is on the naturalistic plane.

Perez Gomar defines international law as

... the application of natural and admitted principles by the civilized and independent nations in order to regulate their differences and to decide conflicts between the laws and usages which govern them [101].

All law, he says, is merely a manifestation of natural law. The same, in his view, is true of civil and political law as well as international law. The dictates of natural law are recognized by the conscience and through "ideas of reason." This state of affairs, in his view, is "the intention of Providence [102]."

This naturalism takes a Pufendorfian turn when Perez observes that the nations which are free and independent, though by themselves having formed a "humanitarian whole," can be ruled only by God [103], an hypothesis which he obviously accepts as sound because, like Pufendorf and not for example like Hobbes, in his next clause he recognizes stability and therefore the actuality of international law [104]. He reiterates that natural law is the only essential basis of law. The conscience and reason by which it is recognized, however, is not that of one person alone, but a recognition that is universal in character. The idea is that by means of general acceptance a rule of natural law is promulgated, not created. He goes on to warn, however, that general acceptance alone does not create an obligatory rule; the rule must of itself be just [105].

---

[101] Gregorio Perez Gomar, *Curso elemental de derecho de gentes* Tomo I (Montevideo, Imprenta tipografia a vapor, 1864) pp. 8–9.
[102] *Ibid.*, pp. 7–8.
[103] *Loc. cit.*
[104] *Ibid.*, p. 16.
[105] *Loc. cit.*

Perhaps the best statement of this author's views appears in the section in which he discusses the sources of international law. The observation is as follows:

We shall not make divisions of international law, because it is the same, but we shall sketch the sources from which it emanates:
1. Directly from reason and universal conscience as the promulgation of eternal justice; some call the law thus recognized *internal*, confusing it with simple moral duty. But the obligation is distinguished from the duty (*deber*), in that the latter may be optional. Thus, as we see it, there is no *imperfect obligation*; every obligation is an unavoidable rule of conduct and one must understand that that which is called imperfect obligation is merely moral duty. All of the obligations of a nation may be required, but not all of its duties.
2. From treaties and conventions, as sources of special obligation. This law is special for the contractors, but it can be invoked in similar cases as demonstration or doctrine. Some call this *positive* law.
3. From the general usages of nations, these usages being just; some call this customary law.
4. Lastly, from the authority of the authors, who as interpreters of the law give legal force to points on which there is agreement, and from the deductions in which the most judicious are in accord [106].

While it is evident that positivist elements play some part in Perez Gomar's system, there would seem to be little doubt that his real orientation is toward naturalism. As to persons or subjects of international law, he seems to be essentially traditional.

JOSÉ SILVA SANTISTEBAN (1825–89), a Peruvian, is another of the many Latin American publicists who wrote his book as a text for teaching. He has written in the areas of constitutional, penal, natural, and international law. The work mentioned here, which was published in 1864, is as close to pure ecclesiastical naturalism as one could hope to find anywhere. While the value of treaties and usages is acknowledged, these are viewed as sterile unless they embody reason and justice [107].

Silva is not entirely clear as to what justice is, but he is persistent in his search. "International law", he says,

---

[106] *Ibid.*, pp. 18–19.
[107] José Silva Santisteban, *Curso de derecho internacional* (Lima, A. Aubert y comp., 1864), pp. 35–36.

... [is] the science which treats of the regulation of international relations according to the eternal principles of justice,
or, in other terms, of the establishment of principles to which
the nations must (*deben*) subject themselves in the granting of
external means necessary for advancing their rational ends [108].

Elsewhere he says that the realization of "the principle of justice" is the end to which nations must direct themselves [109], and
at still another point it is made abundantly clear that natural
law is to be regarded as no less binding in human affairs than
in the realm of physical phenomena. Just as laws govern such
matters as stellar movements, the tides, and the regularity of
night and day, so

... it is undoubtable also that the intelligence obeys unvarying
laws in all the spheres of its activity, and he who would dare
to deny the moral law, would be a stupid person worthy of
pity, a poor blind one who does not see the resplendant light
of truth [110].

These laws apply to nations as well as to men, for, to quote
his own picturesque words,

... the creator of the world who has established the harmony
of the elements, could not have left the nations in chaos; the
God of Israel who led his people in the desert by a mysterious
cloud, likewise has created justice to lead the nations foreward [111].

At a later place is established the relationship which, in Silva's
judgment, obtains between natural and positive law. Accordingly
treaties themselves draw their validity from the natural law.
The meaning is emphatic and clear. There can be no mistaking
the view in the following passage:

But the treaties do not create laws, they are not their source,
but only the social medium for their realization; their obligatory
force, their inviolability and sanctity as one is accustomed to
say, emanate from the pre-existence of the principles of justice
which they verify; a law recognized becomes by the same act
obligatory and inviolable. To search for the obligatory force
of treaties in a preliminary convention, in utility, or in naked
morality, is to mistake the nature of juridical obligation.
For the validity of treaties the same conditions are required

---

[108] *Ibid.*, p. 14.
[109] *Ibid.*, p. 24.
[110] *Ibid.*, p. 12.
[111] *Ibid.*, pp. 12–13.

as are established by natural law for contracts in general, modified somewhat (*un tanto*) by the special nature of the nation; such *requisites* are three: legal capacity, free consent, lawful object [112].

There can be little doubt as to Silva Santisteban's orientation. His naturalism is manifest on virtually every count. It seems quite evident, also, that his views regarding the persons and subjects of international law are traditional.

AUGUSTIN ASPIAZU (1817–97), who has written in the fields of constitutional law and international law, wrote a little text on the latter subject in 1872. This book does not appear to be too well reasoned, yet it has its interesting aspects.

It is not entirely clear just how emphatically Aspiazu embraces naturalism. At one point he sounds almost like Pufendorf; elsewhere he seems to have more of an eclectic flavor.

Although he does not want to dwell at length on the matter, as he considers it of only secondary importance, he concludes that in a scientific sense international law is law only when it conforms to the dictates of justice [113].

At another place, he seems to say that the philosophical or rational international law, while serving as a basis for other aspects of the law of nations, is obligatory on all states, while the conventional law binds only those which agree thereto. Customary law is binding, he thinks, but only so because it is presumed to be in conformity with the dictates of reason; if it does not reflect this ideal, it need not be followed [114].

As to the basis of the binding force of natural law, Aspiazu has the following to say:

The rational law of nations has its obligatory force in the duty of all intelligent and free beings to make their acts conform to the prescriptions of reason and justice. To be just and reasonable is to labor in obedience (*sujecion*) to the judgment of conscience and to the designs of the Creator; to be unjust and arbitrary is to attack another's rights and to make oneself culpable before God and other peoples [115].

An eclecticism appears, however, when it is asked how one

[112] *Ibid.*, p. 89.
[113] Agustin Aspiazu, *Dogmas del derecho internacional* (Nueva York, Imprenta de Hallet and Breen, 1872), p. 3.
[114] *Ibid.*, p. 4.
[115] *Loc. cit.*

would go about determining the just and the rational in any case of doubt, or in a particular "prescription of the conventional law," hence to evaluate its binding effect. He answers by pointing to the sources of international jurisprudence, *i.e.*, to the writers who, when in agreement, make a clear case for the validity of the rule in question [116]. In the section just outlined, Aspiazu mentions conventional law, presumably in the sense of treaty law, and in a passage outlined earlier [117], he speaks of customary law. It is interesting to note that in both instances the idea is that a dictate of neither of these positive forms is valid if it fails to conform to the rational or natural law.

International law is defined as

... the collection of laws or general rules of conduct which states must (*deben*) observe among themselves for their security and common well-being [118].

It seems quite apparent that the main orientation is toward naturalism, although, as has been pointed out, Aspiazu is not without his more positivist facets. His views on the subjects or persons of international law appear to be traditional.

Although the work of ANTONIO SAÉNZ (1780–1825) did not originally appear in book form, it seems not amiss briefly to review his lectures at this point, for it may be conjectured that much pedagogical work of this flavor has been influential in academic and other circles in Latin America. These lectures were given in 1822–3 at the University of Buenos Aires, then only the embryo of the present institution of that name. Saénz, who apparently was a priest and a lawyer as well as a scholar, was rector of the University for a time, and portions of his lecture notes were preserved in the faculty library. In 1939 they were published by the University of Buenos Aires as a contribution to the historiography of Argentine law.

Since much of the work is not extant, a clear picture is hard to draw. Enough is available, however, to indicate a strong naturalistic view.

Drawing a distinction between public law and international

[116] *Ibid.*, pp. 4–5.
[117] *Supra*, fn. 114.
[118] Aspiazu, *op cit.*, p. 7.

law, Saénz points out that the former relates to the interior regulation of the state, while

The law of nations is universal and it comes from nature making itself known (*dandose a conocer*) solely by right reason. Also some are accustomed to call it the original and primitive law of nations. It has obligated and will always obligate all nations and all governments, and it will last as long as the world [119].

Saénz holds that nations exist in a state of nature much like the condition once thought to have been that of individual persons in their pre-civil state, and that their laws

... are derived from an immutable law established by the Author of the Universe, whose precepts are universal, and there is no created being who is not obliged to obey [120].

In defining the law of nations, this complete naturalist observes that

... it is the natural law itself when applied or when taken in the aspect which regulates the social life of man in common, or the business and actions of societies [121].

The virtually complete naturalism of Saénz is apparent. His views on the persons or subjects of international law seem to be traditional.

D. JUAN BAUTISTA ALBERDI

The contribution to international law of the outstanding Argentine, JUAN BAUTISTA ALBERDI (1810–84) has not been particularly lengthy. It is being dealt with separately, however, because it is entirely different in flavor, purpose, and nature from the texts and treatises on international law which have been reviewed up to this point; also because it parallels somewhat and seems almost to anticipate the reform literature of the twentieth century.

Alberdi was not a diplomat like Calvo or Bello, nor a scholar like Alcorta, but a legal, social, and political reformer. He spent much of his life outside his native Argentina because he was

---

[119] Antonio Saénz, *Instituciones elementales sobre el derecho natural y de gentes* [Curso] dictado en la Universidad de Buenos Aires en los años 1822–3 (Buenos Aires, A. Baiocca y cia., 1939), p. 57.

[120] *Ibid.*, p. 56.

[121] *Loc. cit.*

not happily thought of by the authorities there whom he constantly and strongly criticized. Alberdi was especially hard on the dictator, Juan Manuel de Rosas (1793–1877), but after the latter's fall from power in 1852 he returned to Argentina and then served the government in diplomatic capacities in Europe. When a further governmental change occurred in 1861 Alberdi remained abroad. He died in 1884 in Paris.

Alberdi wrote widely, there being some twenty-four volumes to his credit, of which sixteen were published posthumously. It is in these latter works that he makes his suggestions regarding international law. His writings include, however, constitutional matters, international law and relations, economics, sociology, and related matters.

He is probably best known in Argentina for his work, *Las bases*, which is a study of liberal American constitutions and in which he makes some suggestions — destined to be largely accepted — regarding a new Argentine constitution [122].

His reputation and prestige in South America is remarkably high. It might not be amiss to liken him in many respects to Thomas Jefferson in terms of stature and of nineteenth century liberal orientation.

Most of Alberdi's remarks concerning international law are made in his *Crimen de la guerra* [123], although observations on this subject are found scattered throughout other parts of his posthumous works.

With reference to the *Crimen de la guerra*, the whole theme of the work is that war is by all counts an evil and must be abolished, a view which is closely related to his belief that "to govern is to populate [124]." As to the sources of law, Alberdi is fairly explicit. He opines that it is created principally by commerce, "the great peacemaker [125]." It is emphasized, moreover,

---

[122] L. L. Barnard, 'Alberdi, Juan Bautista' *The Encyclopaedia of the Social Sciences* Vol. I (New York, The Macmillan Company, 1937), p. 613. On Alberdi's views on international law generally see Isidoro Ruiz Moreno, *El pensamiento internacional de Alberdi* (Buenos Aires, Imprenta de la Universidad, 1945).

[123] Two separate editions of this work have been used in this study. One is an edition which was published in 1915 and the other constitutes Vol. II of the *Escritos Postumos de J. B. Alberdi*. Each will be appropriately designated when referred to below.

[124] William Rex Crawford, *A Century of Latin-American Thought* (Cambridge, Harvard University Press, 1944), p. 21 *et passim*.

[125] Juan Bautista Alberdi, *El crimen de la guerra* (Buenos Aires, La Cultura Argentina, 1915), p. 90.

that international law is only a segment of the entire body of law as a single unity. "The law", he observes,

is one for all the human race by virtue of the unity itself of the human race.

The unity of law, as the juridical law of man, this is the great and simple foundation on which the whole edifice of human law ought to be constructed [126].

Outlining the several branches of the law, he concludes:

All the confusion and the obscurity, in the perception of a simple and clear law as the moral rule of man, comes from this Olympus or multitude of Gods which live only in the fantasy of the human legislator.

One God, one human species, one law as the law of the human species [127].

"That which is called the *law of nations*", says Alberdi at another place, "is the human law seen in its most general, most elevated, [and] most interesting aspect [128]."

The stress which he places on the unity of law has a certain naturalistic ring about it, and there is considerable evidence to further the point of his reliance on naturalism. Only war, he suggests, is a justification for war [129]; and again, war is by nature partial and hence unjust [130]; and elsewhere, "... war is a crime when it does not have peace for [its] object, that is to say, justice, which is the basis and condition of peace [131]."

At another place it is said that

... the law which is used for natural law in order to regulate the relations of man to man within the nation, is one and the same as that which regulates the relations of nation to nation [132].

In a similar though more exhortative vein he urges the creation of a more cohesive world society which will result naturally in a legal system, *i.e.*, *ubi societas ibi jus*.

The authors of international law are not those who have developed international law.

---

[126] *Ibid.*, p. 70.
[127] *Ibid.*, p. 71.
[128] *Ibid.*, pp. 71–72.
[129] *Ibid.*, p. 50.
[130] *Ibid.*, c.p. 42.
[131] Juan Bautista Alberdi, 'Memorias y documentos', *Escritos postumos de J. B. Alberdi* Tomo XV (Buenos Aires, Imprenta Juan Bautista Alberdi, 1900), p. 35.
[132] Alberdi, *El crimen de la guerra* 1915 edition, p. 75.

In order to develop international law as a science, in order to give it as law the dominion of the world, what matters is to create the international material, the international substance, the international life, that is to say, the union of the nations into a vast social body of so many heads of states, governed by a thought, by an opinion, by a universal and common judge. The law will come by itself as the law of life of this body [133].

There is, on the other hand, a phase of Alberdi's writing which sounds somewhat like James Mill [134] or Hugo Krabbe [135] or even to a degree like Jean Spiropolous [136]. This is where he emphasizes the importance of public opinion. After remarking with reference to the lack of a judge to decide international problems, he suggests that the absence of such an authority does not, however, preclude the possibility of a general opinion or consensus on any given problem [137]. Even here, however, one has the feeling that Alberdi does not cast aside his naturalism, but rather that public opinion in some way reflects justice *per se*.

Since this opinion exists, or is possible, international law and the justice pronounced according to it, are possible, because among nations as among individuals, in the world society as in the national society, law is nought but the expression of the general opinion, and the superior judicial judgment is that which concurs completely with the public conscience [138].

Suffice it to say here that this material as a whole suggests a strongly naturalistic eclecticism in international law, but it is an eclecticism which reflects not so much the customary Latin American reliance on a form of ecclesiastical naturalism, as a reliance on something akin to nineteenth century rationalism.

Regarding the persons or subjects of international law, Alberdi, while not altogether clear, nevertheless is sufficiently so to indicate a remarkable modernism. "... the objects of international law", he says,

are the same as those of civil law: *persons*, that is to say, *States*, considered in their sovereign condition; things, that is to say, territories, seas, rivers, mountains, etc., considered in themselves and in their relations with the States which acquire possess

---

[133] *Ibid.*, p. 92.
[134] *Supra*, p. 26.
[135] *Supra*, p. 33.
[136] *Supra*, p. 35.
[137] Alberdi, *El crimen de la guerra*, 1915 edition, p. 69.
[138] *Loc. cit.*

and transfer them, that is to say, treaties, conventions, cessions, inheritances, etc. [139].

It is to be observed that Alberdi speaks in the last paragraph of "objects" of international law and not subjects. Whether this distinction has relevancy here is perhaps an open question [140], but certain other statements would seem to resolve the question in the negative. An example may be seen in the following unusual remark:

The favorite persons of international law are States; but as these are composed of men, the person of the man is not foreign to international law.
Not only the states are members of humanity as society, but the individuals of which the states are composed.
In the the last analysis the individual man is the elemental unity of all human associations; and all law, though it be collective and general, is ultimately resolved in a law of man [141].

Somewhat later in the same discussion Alberdi makes the following remark which, considering the century in which it was written, is almost startling as representing a viewpoint which even today is sufficiently rare:

... when one or many individuals of a state are injured as regards their international rights, that is to say, as members of the society of humanity, although it be by the government of their country, they can invoke international law, to ask the world to make it respect their persons even though it be against the government of their own country.
The intervention which they ask, they do not ask in the name of the state: only the government is the organ to speak in the name of the state. They ask it in their own name through international law which protects them in the guarantees of liberty, life, security, equality, etc. [142].

---

[139] *Ibid.*, pp. 87–88.
[140] Charles G. Fenwick, *International Law* (New York, Appleton-Century-Crofts, Inc., 1948), p. 129. Fenwick notes that: "'Subject,' as the term is used in general jurisprudence, are the persons to whom the law attributes rights and duties; 'objects' are the things in respect to which rights are held and duties imposed." *Cf. loc. cit.* n. 116 where he says: "But many writers use the terms 'subjects,' 'persons,' 'international personality', without careful distinctions, with the result that some writers may be cited on both sides of the controversy."
[141] Juan Bautista Alberdi, 'El crimen de la guerra', *Escritos postumos de J. B. Alberdi* Tomo II (Buenos Aires, Imprenta Europea, Moreno y Defensa, 1895), p. 157.
[142] *Ibid.*, p. 158. *Cf.* also Crawford, *op. cit.*, p. 31 where Alberdi is cited as advocating the punishment of those responsible for a nation's guilt. This certainly anticipates the Nuremberg Trials and is another evidence of Alberdi's modernity.

Although Alberdi's views on the nature of international law can best be labeled as strongly naturalistic eclecticism, it is nevertheless true that the overpowering consideration — toward which, it must be emphasized, he was directing his argument — was the power of public opinion. He was out to make changes and in so doing he used both naturalistic and positivistic elements, but his importance rests largely on what he was trying to accomplish, *i.e.*, the abolition of war.

As to his conception of the persons of international law, he alone among nineteenth century Latin American writers views the individual in the light of having international personality. In this regard he anticipated one of the most momentous of twentieth century developments in the field of international law.

E. MISCELLANY

In addition to the writers who have been reviewed above in some detail, a few titles should be mentioned in the interest of making this chapter as complete a survey of the nineteenth century literature in this area as is possible.

Among these works is *Derecho internacional mexicano* [143], a work in three volumes which is sometimes ascribed to ANGEL NUÑEZ ORTEGA, but which was apparently compiled by several persons under his direction. Although its title sounds pertinent, it is actually an official compilation of treaties, unratified treaties, and pertinent laws.

A similar work is *Derecho internacional guatemalteco* [144] ascribed to D. RAMON SALAZAR and FEDERICO S. DE TEJADA. This too is a three-volume work, volumes two and three of which were published in 1912 and 1919 respectively and strictly speaking, therefore, do not deserve mention in this chapter. This work, like its Mexican prototype, is merely a compilation of Guatemalan treaties. In addition, a work thought to be by Federico S. de Tejada entitled *Derecho internacional*, 1894, was sought but could not be located, and it is conjectured that this latter title

[143] Angel Nuñez Ortega, *Derecho internacional mexicano* (Mexico, Imprenta de Gonzalo A. Esteve, 1878, — Partes I y II; Tipografia literaria de Filomeno Mata, 1879 — Parte III) 3 partes (vols.).

[144] D. Ramon Salazar and Federico S. de Tejada, *Derecho internacional guatemaltico* (Guatemala, Tipografia y encuadernación 'nacional', 1892, 1912, and 1919), 3 vols.

may have been merely an incorrect citation of *Derecho internacional guatemalteco*.

The two works which have just been mentioned are by their very nature such as to add emphasis to the positivist tradition.

Another title which at first seemed pertinent is *International Law of Spanish America* [145] by DON ESTANISLAO S. ZEBALLOS (1854–1923) which was published in 1893. This work, though by its title seeming to be applicable to a study such as this, is merely a statement opposing Brazil's position on the Misiones dispute.

Elementos de derecho natural y de gentes [146], written by the priest, CIRIACO MORELLI (1718–95), who was at the University of Cordoba was translated in the third volume of the faculty studies of the National University of La Plata by Dr. Luciano Abeille. It appeared in 1911. It seems to be an ecclesiastical statement of natural law and of its application to international law. It was felt that this work was not within the scope of the materials to be covered.

The general work of Henry Wheaton which was cited in the first chapter of this study [147] was translated into Spanish by the Mexican, José María Barros [148]. Since Wheaton's work was mentioned earlier in this survey, and since it is comparatively well-known to American students of international law, it was felt that its perusal here would not be profitable.

A work by JUAN DE LA TORRE entitled *Guia para el estudio del derecho internacional de Mexico* and reputedly published in 1879 was not available, but a tome bearing the same bibliographical data was available under the title of *Guia para el estudio del derecho constitutional mexicano* [149]. It is surmised that the former title was a misprint and that no such work exists.

In addition, there were a number of works of the type reviewed

---

[145] Don Estanislao S. Zeballos, *International Law of Spanish America; Arbitration on Misiones* (Buenos Aires, Jacobo Peuser, 1893).

[146] Ciriaco Morelli, *Elementos de derecho natural y de gentes*, 1791 edition (Translated from Latin into Spanish by Luciano Abeillo; Buenos Aires, Imprenta de Coni Hermanos, 1911). Ciriaco Morelli is a pseudonym for Domingo Muriel.

[147] *Supra*, Chapter I, fn. 76.

[148] José María Barros, *Elementos de derecho internacional por Henry Wheaton* (Mexico, Impr. de J. M. Lara, 1854–5), 2 vols.

[149] Juan de la Torre, *Guia para el estudio del derecho constiucional mexicano* (Mexico, Tip. de J. V. Villada, 1886).

in this survey which, though nineteenth century products of Latin America, could not be located for perusal. These are the following:

Acosta y Lara, Federico, *Apuntes para un curso de derecho internacional público*. (Uruguay, 1896).

Alçandara, Bellagarde, *Noçoes elementos de direito das gentes*. (Brazil, 1851).

Azcárate, *El derecho internacional americano*. (1898).

Gaenaga, Magnasco, y Echaida, *Notas sobre el derecho internacional público y privado*. (Argentina, 1883).

Leguizamón, Onésimo, *Apuntes sobre el programa oficial del primer curso*, tomados por Luis T. Pintos y Joaquín Rivadavia. (Argentina, 1874).

Luna, Antonio, *Manual del estudiante sobre derecho internacional*. (Argentina, 1884).

Martinez Silva, Carlos, *Notas a la obra de Bello*. (Colombia, 1883).

Matta, Pedro da Autram e Albuquerque, *Elementos de direito das gentes*. (Brazil, 1851).

Montefar, Lorenzo, *Nociones de derecho de gentes y leyes de la guerra*. (Guatemala, 1893).

Pereira, Pinto, *Apuntomentos para o direito internacional*. (Brazil, 1864).

Pinto, Luis T., Rivadavia, Joaquín, y Leguizamón, Onésimo, *Derecho internacional*. (Argentina, 1894). (This title and that of Leguizamón listed above may refer to the same work).

Suárez, *Compendio de derecho internacional de don Andrés Bello*. (Chile, 1883).

Conclusions

From the preceding analysis of certain theoretical aspects of nineteenth century Latin American writers of international law, a number of fairly clear conclusions can be drawn.

1. First, it must be concluded that there are relatively few absolutists who speak either in terms of pure positivism or of pure naturalism. All of the authors with perhaps the exception of Silva Santisteban and Antonio Saénz are eclectics in some

degree. It is significant in this respect that six of the general treatise writers together with Alberdi were placed in this category.

2. The second of these conclusions is that the positivist strain was probably the most influential of the three, and that the most highly respected writers of the nineteenth century were of this persuasion. Of the writers reviewed, five were classified under this heading and the two border-line authors, Tremosa y Nadal and Bourdon-Viane, were also of this persuasion. It is evident, of course, that none of these positivists were absolutists; rather, their orientation can best be summed up in the following quotation from the noted Argentine, Carlos Calvo:

For our part, we recognize that the general ideal of justice can modify the relations of states to their well-being and common profit; nevertheless in the course of our work, we shall attach preference to principles defined by treaties, to rules which are deduced naturally and logically from particular conventions or from diverse instances resolved in practice, finally to sanctioned jurisprudence [150].

3. In opposition to the positivist strain which was in evidence in both the positivist and the eclectic writers, there was also a less pronounced, but nevertheless important naturalistic thread which runs through many nineteenth century works. The best example of this point of view in a relatively pure form is the book by Silva Santisteban, but the eclectic works also display evidences of this type of thinking. In addition to the class notes of Antonio Saénz, works of four of the authors surveyed were classified as naturalistic. There is evidence presented elsewhere to the effect that this naturalistic strain has both neo-Kantian and neo-scholastic elements [151], but no attempt has been made here to determine these points of origin.

4. With the sole exception of Juan Bautista Alberdi, there is no deviation from the traditional position that the subjects of international law are states and no other parties [152]. Alberdi's position, however, anticipates one of the most active and interesting questions of twentieth century international law.

---

[150] Calvo, *op. cit.*, p. 154.

[151] Josef L. Kunz, *Latin-American Philosophy of Law in the Twentieth Century*.

[152] The question of the international personality of the Vatican has not been considered in this survey.

5. It would appear that the Latin American orientation reflected in general the same trends as were evident in the rest of the world during the nineteenth century. There is, however, sufficient evidence to indicate that Latin American jurists have entertained slightly more naturalistic elements in their thinking than was true throughout the world as a whole. This, as has been said, is a matter of slight degree only.

CHAPTER III

THE WRITERS OF THE TWENTIETH CENTURY

Introduction

This chapter, without making any attempt to exhaust the literature, is based on a study of certain selected texts and treatises among which are the works of the more widely known writers. In addition, selected examples of the new international law are reviewed.

The plan followed in Part I has been to group the positivists and eclectics separately without the additional category for naturalism that was included in the previous chapter. This is because there has been less evidence of relatively pure naturalism in the last five decades than before, so that the only useful division would seem to be the one employed.

Part II of this chapter is devoted not to writers of treatises on international law in general, but to advocates of the new international law. It has been observed elsewhere in this study that during the twentieth century there has been a marked reaction against the excesses of positivism [1], and the Latin American segment of this movement has been remarkably active. Within it are to be found works of considerable interest, a number of which will be reviewed in some detail, and a few others mentioned with a view to indicating trends.

Part I

A. THE POSITIVISTS

LAFAYETTE RODRIGUEZ PEREIRA (1839–1917) was a Brazilian writer whose literary endeavor encompassed family law, private

---

[1] *Supra*, pp. 33–37.

international law, and other legal studies as well as public international law.

"International law," he notes, in his *Principios de direito internacional* [2], "comes to be the complex of the principles which regulate the rights and obligations of the nations among themselves [3]."

He makes an introductory remark that this work "... is a book of positive law and not of philosophical law", but that "The philosophical element is not forgotten", observing that he invokes the latter to "... explain the cause or the reason of a principle ...", to fill lacunae, to indicate criteria for a critique of accepted doctrines, or to suggest reforms [4].

In this vein, he clearly states his view that there is a law higher than the positive law. Of this he says:

There exists, certainly, above the positive international law an ideal law which science conceives of as pure theory whether as an aggregate of metaphysical concepts of reason or as a high generalization of juridical facts [5].

He then observes that this natural or philosophical law has a threefold relationship to international law: "... it influences its formation, it furnishes elements for its comprehension, and it gives criteria for its criticism and betterment [6]."

The moral principle is not *ipso facto* the law, however. Consent is the means by which law is developed out of the moral sphere. Of this he says:

The principle which is not recognized by the procedure of the nations, nor admitted and accepted by their consent, does not have obligatory force for them in the external world, however just the reasons on which it is based may be [7].

As to the sources of international law at one place he mentions tradition, history, public documents, pacts, and conventions adding that treatises of the publicists though lacking legal authority have their influence [8]. Elsewhere, he distinguishes be-

---

[2] Lafayette Rodriguez Pereira, *Principios de direito internacional* (Rio de Janeiro, Jacintho Ribeiro dos Santos, 1902–3). 2 vols.

[3] *Ibid.*, Vol. I, p. 2.

[4] *Ibid.*, p. V.

[5] *Ibid.*, p. 26.

[6] *Loc. cit.*

[7] *Ibid.*, p. 24.

[8] *Ibid.*, p. 3.

tween sources and media. The former are the acts "... by which the [human] will creates the judicial principle ...", and the latter are the documents which "... establish the existence ..." of the sources. Recognition, usage and custom, and public treaties and conventions are cited as constituting the sources of positive international law [9]. Both of these categories are manifestly positivist.

It would seem fair to judge this work as essentially positivist. It is evident also that the author's conception of persons or subjects of international law is traditional.

JOSÉ FLORES Y FLORES (1866–1908), a Guatemalan professor who wrote a text in 1902 for classroom use [10], defines international law in the traditional way. He seems not to attempt a definition of his own, but quotes several authorities. His view resembles that of Calvo or Bello [11]. International law is derived from the coexistence of states [12]. The basis of the scientific system of international law, he points out while quoting Torres Campos, is the concept of the international community [13].

A true picture of international law, however, is not to be seen without the usual dichotomy of natural and positive law. The former "... is the natural law of the coexistence of states. ..." It is grounded on the necessary relations deduced from the coexistence of states, and also on the omnipresent necessity of every state to preserve its own essential characteristics and to respect those of others. The latter, i.e., the positive law "... rests on the consent of the [states] ... shown expressly by reciprocal agreement or tacitly by constant observance [14]."

There are two references to sources which seem to have some relevancy. In the one place he makes an interesting observation concerning Ortolan, a Spanish writer, who classifies the sources of international law under the three categories of reason, customs, and public treaties. Of the first Ortolan says that it is reason by which man acquires the knowledge of what is just and unjust. However, Flores suggests, in agreement with Ortolan

---

[9] *Ibid.*, p. 5.
[10] José Flores y Flores, *Extracto de derecho internacional* (Guatemala, Tipografia nacional, 1902).
[11] *Ibid.*, pp. 38–39. *Cf. supra*, pp. 42, 45.
[12] *Ibid.*, p. 38.
[13] *Ibid.*, p. 40.
[14] *Ibid.*, p. 57.

himself, that in order to give this classification practical application, the priority must be reversed to read 1. treaties, 2. customs, and 3. principles [15]. This contrast between the viewpoints of theoretical observation and practical application in such clear form is not often encountered.

At another place he mentions the following as sources: universal morality, history, diplomatic correspondence, opinions of the jurisconsults, the decisions of mixed courts, laws and mercantile regulations, the related sciences (*e.g.*, civil law, political economy, *etc.*), treaties and conventions, usages, practices, customs, principles of Roman law, and the works of the publicists [16].

It is apparent that Flores y Flores has a moderately positivistic inclination. It seems also that he has a traditional attitude toward the persons and subjects of international law.

ISIDORO RUIZ MORENO (1876–   ) is an Argentine and one of the better known contemporary Latin American writers in the field of international law, whose work reviewed here was published in 1934 [17].

There is no statement in which Ruiz Moreno clearly establishes his views on the basic nature of international law. While he suggests that he would support naturalism to a limited degree, he fears it as being generally too flexible [18]. To positivism, he gives a certain support, but feels that it, too, is only a part of the over all picture [19]. Later, while he does not clearly state his view, the reader is given the impression that eclecticism has his real support [20].

Ruiz Moreno remarks that in the view of some writers the term source (*fuente*) signifies a "means of manifestation", but for the majority, among whom he places himself, it suggests "... the origin from which the law stems." These sources, he observes, are to be classified as direct and indirect. The former include customs, conventions, decisions of the League of Nations as regards its members, and international jurisprudence. The

---

[15] *Ibid.*, p. 77.
[16] *Ibid.*, pp. 69–76.
[17] Isidoro Ruiz Moreno, *Lecciones de derecho internacional publico* (Buenos Aires, El ateneo, 1934–5) 3 vols.
[18] *Ibid.*, Vol. I, pp. 17–18.
[19] *Ibid.*, pp. 18–19.
[20] *Ibid.*, pp. 19–20.

latter embrace national law, the opinion of persons of insight (*instintos*) who study the matter, the opinion of the internationalists, and public opinion [21].

At another place he speaks of rights as existing anterior to law and says that certain writers confuse the terms rights (*derechos*) and laws (*leyes*) when they suggest that only natural laws may be said to exist as regulating international life [22].

By way of definition he would say that:

... public international law is the aggregate of principles and rules which govern the relations among international persons and among the states, and the international rights and duties of individuals [23].

As for what entities have international personality, he observes that this category has been extended since the nineteenth century; specifically he mentions states, confederations, the League of Nations, certain colonies, the Papacy, belligerent communities, the Straits Commission, the Permanent Court of International Justice, the International Court of Arbitration, and other international commissions [24]. Although some authors consider individuals as persons before international law, to this he would not agree, noting that when individuals appear before international courts — even mixed tribunals — the states are the real parties [25].

There is some reason to consider this writer as an eclectic, yet it would seem that his real inclinations are positivistic. For example, among the sources which he regards as basic in character and not merely as manifestations of the law, he mentions only positivist elements—unless there be a degree of naturalistic implication in the indirect source which he terms "... the opinion of persons of insight who study the matter ... [26]." In the light of this analysis, it appears that Ruiz Moreno should be classed among the positivists.

As to the persons of international law, he expresses quite a modern view. Individuals, however, do not merit international

[21] *Ibid.*, p. 20.
[22] *Ibid.*, p. 12.
[23] *Ibid.*, p. 9.
[24] *Ibid.*, p. 83.
[25] *Ibid.*, p. 84.
[26] *Supra*, f. 22.

personality. On the other hand, individuals apparently are seen as having some international rights and duties. Consequently, it would seem that his remarks are somewhat contradictory.

CECILIO BÁEZ (1862–1941), a former president of Paraguay and a professional diplomat, a professor of law and of social sciences at the National University of Asunción as well as its rector for a time, among his extensive publications, wrote a little text in 1936 which is of modest interest to this study [27].

He does not himself attempt to define international law, but quotes the essentially traditional definitions of J. de Louter, L. Oppenheim, and Von Liszt.

International persons are, according to his mention at one place, the League of Nations, dominions, colonies, natural persons, ethnic and other minorities, the Permanent Court of International Justice, international banks, and mandates in addition, of course, to states [28]. Elsewhere he says that "States are the only subjects of international law capable of international rights and obligations [29]." He goes on to observe, however, that a trend exists to allow to other entities the enjoyment of a degree of personality in the international sphere. The individual, he suggests may have limited personality, but not to the extent of having rights [30]. His closing remark on this subject is a reaffirmation of the view that only states are subjects of international law [31].

As to the foundation and sources of international law, Báez feels that the "ethical-juridical concience of peoples" is the foundation (he uses the term *fuentes* or sources, but he seems to mean foundation) of international law. This phenomenon "... gives obligatory character to the economic and moral rules emerging from the mutual relationship (*la vida de relacion*), [*i.e.*,] from solidarity [32]." Customs and treaties express that conscience [33].

At another place he observes that international law is positive

---

[27] Cecilio Báez, *Derecho internacional publico europea y americano* (Asunción, Imprenta nacional, 1936).
[28] *Ibid.*, pp. 6–7.
[29] *Ibid.*, p. 99.
[30] *Ibid.*, pp. 99–100.
[31] *Ibid.*, p. 101.
[32] *Ibid.*, p. 22.
[33] *Loc. cit.*

law and that its obligatory nature stems from the will of states [34]. Again, he says that customs and treaties are its only sources [35], observing that general principles of justice are really customs [36], and that while the opinions of writers influence the unfolding of international law, these are not a true source of the law of nations [37].

Thus, it is fairly apparent that Báez' position on the persons of international law is essentially traditional, and that his philosophical orientation is positivist.

RAUL PARANHOS PEDERNEIRAS (1874–   ) is a Brazilian writer and professor of remarkable versatility whose work on international law has gone through nine editions. His sixth or 1938 edition has been used in this survey [38].

The work seems vague in some respects, and the author apparently makes no attempt to define his discipline.

Principles for the regulation of the relations among states, when they are made positive by means of reciprocal consent, establish, in Pederneiras' view, a composite of norms of juridical activity [39].

Necessity is the foundation of international law. Of this he says:

The basis of international law, in our view, is found in *necessity* [which is the] only reason for the existence of relations among individuals or communities of individuals. Necessity united to the collective will or, at least, the will of two (*dual*), [being] the only sanction of these relations [40].

As to the principal sources of international law, Pederneiras mentions agreements, customs, and treaties (apparently this includes the resolutions of the League of Nations). Regarding subsidiary sources, he lists the individual laws of states, jurisprudence, the work of jurists, diplomatic acts, history, Roman law, the Hague conventions (presumably in a suggestive and advisory capacity where they have not been adhered to), public

---

[34] *Ibid.*, p. 93.
[35] *Ibid.*, p. 94.
[36] *Ibid.*, p. 96.
[37] *Ibid.*, p. 97.
[38] Raul Pederneiras, *Direito internacional compendiado* (Rio de Janeiro, A. Coelho Branco, 1938).
[39] *Ibid.*, p. 21.
[40] *Ibid.*, p. 31.

opinion, the codifications, the national and international societies of international law, and monographs of creditable writers [41].

Pederneiras' orientation is toward positivism. His remarks are inconclusive as regards the persons of international law, but he seems to be essentially traditional in this respect.

One of the most interesting writers of the twentieth century is the Mexican, FRANCISCO A. URSÚA (1894–   ) who published his work in 1938 [42]. The book was designed to be used as a text or for similar purposes [43].

Ursúa observes that the term source (*fuente*) is really not applicable to treaties, customs, court decisions, or the writers of international law. He suggests that these elements are merely proofs [44]. The foundation of juridical activity, however, is society itself, and he feels that this belief is accepted everywhere. More specifically he finds it necessary to relate juridical activity to "... the notion of necessary reciprocity which ..." is to be found "at the bottom of all juridical ideas [45]." "The norm of law considered objectively", he goes on to say,

is nothing, in reality, but the expression of this same norm existing subjectively in the bosom (*seno*) of humanity or of the group which is considered; it ought to be, then, in itself the basis of a classification of [legal] matters, to the end of not losing sight of its genesis [which is an] essential and indispensable part of its real content [46].

He considers that one should speak not of the fundamentals of a science so much as of the study of a collective phenomenon, *i.e.*, the cooperative force (*sinergia*) of natural manifestations acting in accordance with the laws of the organs which produce them. These organs in this case are human societies [47].

As to the nature of law, he observes that:

The *concept of law* is then, as a materialistic reality, the *collective social conscience of a directive force which embraces the relations*

---

[41] *Ibid.*, pp. 47–55.
[42] Francisco A. Ursúa, *Derecho internacional publico* (Mexico, Editorial 'Cultura,' 1938).
[43] *Ibid.*, p. XIX.
[44] *Ibid.*, pp. XVII–XVIII and 41–42.
[45] *Ibid.*, p. XVI.
[46] *Loc. cit.*
[47] *Ibid.*, p. 9.

*which are subject, by virtue of a conscious generalization, to a
necessary reciprocity among all the members of the community
which it governs* [48].

Speaking of international law, he merely says that:

*... international law is the collective social conscience of a directive
force which embraces the relations which are subject, by virtue of
a conscious generalization, to a necessary reciprocity among all
the members of humanity, when these relations go beyond the limits
of state jurisdiction or are in themselves of an interstatal nature* [49].

As to the persons of international law, he has the three classifications of (1) subjects of international law including individuals, moral persons, and ethnic groups, (2) international
subjects of law including the League of Nations, the Papacy,
and international commissions, and (3) persons of international
law, *i.e.*, states, which are held to enjoy perfect juridical personality [50].

From this evidence it would seem that Ursúa is a follower
of Duguit, *i.e.*, a sociological positivist. It is evident, also, that
while he does not follow Duguit to the point of designating
individuals as the only real subjects of international law, he is,
nevertheless, well within the modern tradition in that he greatly
expands the scope of international law and puts the individual
in a place where he at least gets some recognition.

CLOVIS BEVILAQUA (1859–1944) was one of the leading Brazilian publicists of this century. His writings have included
public and private international law and other legal subjects.
The second edition of his treatise, *Direito publico internacional*,
published in 1939, was used in this survey [51]. The work was
written to show the main principles of public international law
as reflected in Brazilian practice [52].

Bevilaqua, drawing on the many definitions which he finds
in Sá Vianna's work, believes that they can all be reduced to
this: "... public international law is that which regulates the
relations of states among themselves [53]."

---

[48] *Ibid.*, p. 26.
[49] *Ibid.*, p.36.
[50] *Ibid.*, pp. 68–69.
[51] Clovis Bevilaque, *Direito publico internacional* (Rio de Janeiro, Freitas Bastos,
1939) 2 vols.
[52] *Ibid.*, Vol. I, p. VII.
[53] *Ibid.*, p. 15.

Confirming what this definition suggests regarding the status of persons, he views only states and the Holy See as enjoying international personality [54].

Regarding the foundations of international law, he speaks of solidarity rather than of sovereignty as the basic stratum out of which international law arises [55].

As to sources, he is essentially a positivist. He adopts the classification of Cavaglieri who says that confusion exists as between the nature of sources and of evidences of international law. The latter include such elements as court decisions and government acts; but the only real sources are customs and treaties [56].

It is apparent that Clovis Bevilaqua's views on international personality are traditional, and that his philosophical orientation is positivistic.

One of the leading contemporary Argentine publicists is DANIEL ANTOKOLETZ (1881–   ) whose writings, diplomatic activities, and professional experience have thoroughly qualified him in the field of international law. The fourth edition of his treatise published in 1944 has been used in this survey [57].

Antokoletz defines public international law as the

... *aggregate of theoretical principles, practical rules, and moral norms applicable, not only among states, but also between states and associations of states, and in relations of these among themselves, and with other international persons* [58].

As to persons of international law, he notes that states though not the only international persons, are the chief ones [59]. Among the others he mentions the Papacy, the League of Nations, the Pan American Union, the European Danube Commission, and certain autonomous dominions [60]. He does not feel that the inidividual is an international person [61].

Turning to the nature of international law, Antokoletz finds

[54] *Ibid.*, pp. 31–205.
[55] *Ibid.*, p. 11.
[56] *Ibid.*, pp. 24–25.
[57] Daniel Antokoletz, *Tratado de derecho internacional publico* (Buenos Aires, Bernabe y cía, 1944) 3 vols.
[58] *Ibid.*, Vol. I, p. 14.
[59] *Ibid.*, p. 471.
[60] *Ibid.*, p. 473.
[61] *Ibid.*, p. 475.

its foundations in the need for states to live together and in the consequent juridical relationship exemplified in the adage *"ubi societas ibi jus* [62].*"*

The sources of international law are much confused, he opines, but after a long discussion of the various writers' views, he lists in order of importance: *positive sources* embracing treaties, customs, general principles, and international court decisions; and *doctrinal sources* including consultative decisions of the Permanent Court of International Justice, European and American codification projects in the League of Nations or the Pan American Union, dictates of the scientific institutions, and the opinions of classical and contemporary writers [63].

Antokoletz makes the usual distinction between natural and positive law. He is of the opinion that often the two do not coincide in that the ideal is ahead of reality. The implication is that natural law constitutes an intellectual conception of what ought to be, while positive law (expressly or tacitly agreed to by states) stipulates the actual law [64].

Although Antokoletz shows some deference to natural law, it appears that his basic orientation is positivistic. It is also apparent that his views on international personality are essentially traditional.

One of the most recent classroom textbooks on international law is the little work published in 1946 by the Ecuadoran, TEODORO ALVARADO GARAICOA (1903–   ) [65].

As to definition he quotes Sanchez de Bustamente, Fiore, Bello, Alcorta, Antokoletz, and For, all of whom take traditional views [66]. On the other hand, when speaking elsewhere of the subjects of international law, he observes that where the states used to be the only entities so considered, now "... the Church, mandates, some political groups, and international entities such as the British Commonwealth of Nations, the Universal Postal Union and lastly, the individual" are also within this classification [67]. This is modified somewhat at another place where he

---

[62] *Ibid.*, pp. 38–39, 121–122.
[63] *Ibid.*, p. 54.
[64] *Ibid.*, p. 17.
[65] Teodoro Alvarado Garaicoa, *Principios normativos del derecho internacional publico* (Guayaquil, Impr. de la Universidad, 1946).
[66] *Ibid.*, pp. 15–17.
[67] *Ibid.*, p. 189.

observes that the individual is occasionally a person in international law [68].

As to the sources of international law, he mentions certain national laws, jurisprudence (apparently court decisions based largely on morality and equity), custom, treaties, and the doctrines of the writers of note [69]. Of these custom is " . . . perhaps the source par excellence of international law [70]."

The chief orientation here is that of positivism. As to subjects of international law, his view is clearly not the traditional one as he includes the individual person in at least some instances.

Probably the most famous contemporary Latin American authority on international law is the Cuban, ANTONIO SANCHEZ DE BUSTAMENTE Y SIRVEN (1865–1951). His attendance at international conferences, membership in international law associations, professorial record, writings, and especially his judgeship on the Permanent Court of International Justice have made him one of the world's best known and most highly respected jurists. The fourth edition of his *Manual de derecho international publico* published in 1947 has been used for this survey [71].

Bustamente y Sirven defines public international law as

. . . the aggregate of principles which regulate the exterior rights and duties and the relations of the juridical persons which form part of the international community, among themselves and with collective international organizations and the Pan American Union, likewise the common norms of internal or external individual protection established by international accords [72].

The entities to be considered as juridical persons, he observes, are those civilized human societies which exercise sovereignty over territory, and that have their own organized governments with which to control foreign representation and international trade. He notes that this does not exclude everything but the recognized nation state, and mentions as examples of additional subjects of international law the virtually sovereign British

---

[68] *Ibid.*, pp. 199–200.
[69] *Ibid.*, pp. 30–32.
[70] *Ibid.*, p. 30.
[71] Antonio Sanchez de Bustamente y Sirven, *Manual de derecho internacional publico* (La Habana, La 'Mercantil,' 1947).
[72] *Ibid.*, p. 9.

Dominions [73]. The individual, however, while often the object of international law is never its direct subject [74].

Bustamente is careful to distinguish between the foundation and sources of international law. The former is that element without which international law itself would never have had cause for being, whereas the latter is either the immediate fabricator or a mere evidence of the law [75].

The foundation of international law, he explains is the community itself in which the state exists as directed toward the juridical end of a mutual maintenance of rights and duties [76].

This law rests, and must necessarily rest, on the juridical community of international persons; but the juridical community always is organized and maintained not as the destroyer [this term could also be translated as "consumer"] but as the guarantee of reciprocal and equal rights and duties of each and all of its component elements [77].

Bustamente makes an interesting distinction between "generative" and "evidential" sources of international law. The former, although to be distinguished from foundations, are the immediate loci from which the rules of international law spring. Examples are custom in its formative aspects, pertinent national legislative, judicial and executive acts, and science which includes the writings of the jurists, the works of scientific associations, and professorial declamations. The direct consequences of such as these add up to the general principles of law. Also, the acts of the League of Nations, permanent American conferences, special conferences, together with international court decisions are to be considered as generative sources.

Among the evidential sources mentioned are custom (as already known and in force), pertinent diplomatic correspondence and negotiations, national and international legislation especially treaties and conventions, and national and international jurisprudence, *i.e.*, court decisions [78].

Bustamente y Sirven is essentially traditional regarding the

---

[73] *Ibid.*, p. 19.
[74] *Ibid.*, p. 22.
[75] *Ibid.*, p. 13.
[76] *Ibid.*, pp. 13–14.
[77] *Ibid.*, p. 14.
[78] *Loc. cit.*

persons of international law. As to the theory of international law, he mentions three levels: (1) the ultimate foundations of international law, (2) the immediate generative sources of international law, and (3) the evidences of international law. In all of these the position is fundamentally positivist.

B. THE ECLECTICS

D. RAMON RIBEYRO, a Peruvian writer and professor, published a work which is essentially a résumé of class lectures on international law. It appeared in 1901 with a second volume following in 1905 [79].

Ribeyro makes much of the usual dichotomy of natural and positive branches of international law. "Natural reason and moral perception", he says, "do not permit us to confuse what is essentially just and good, with what is unjust and bad [80]." With the aid of these powers, man has been able to construct a code which in effect sets the "rational limit" to the exercise of his "exterior liberty." Of all this he says: "I have here the philosophical element of the law of nations founded in a principle preëxistent and superior to human will and as such immutable [81]".

On the other hand there are, however, numerous degrees of human perfection and many divergent needs along with "unstable situations and transitory conditions." The positive obligations, then, are based on utility and convenience.

I have here the second element to which we have referred and which it is not possible to abbreviate [if one is] to give a complete notion of international law and of the science which it explains [82].

Ribeyro defines international law as follows:

From here we conclude that international law *is the aggregate of rational rules and of positive institutions which govern the relations of nations among themselves in peace and war and which have for their object the resolving of conflicts* [83].

---

[79] D. Ramon Ribeyro, *Derecho internacional publico* (Lima, Imprenta de E. Moreno, 1901–5) 2 vols.
[80] *Ibid.*, Vol. I, p. 7.
[81] *Loc. cit.*
[82] *Loc. cit.*
[83] *Loc. cit.*

There is much naturalism in the writing of Ribeyro. He makes a point of observing how impossible it would be to conceive of the order in the universe were it not for natural or physical law. This applies also to the "moral world" and to "the coexistence of free beings [84]." It is quite logical, then, for international law to be based very largely on a "supreme and eternal intelligence [85]."

"The positive laws (*leyes*)", he says at another place, "are nothing but the most clear and defined expressions of the ideal law (*derecho*) ... [86]." And elsewhere after remarking that sanction is not the essence of the law, but only a complementary factor, it is noted that

The law is such by conforming with the conception of justice and by the fact of having been dictated by the authority of God and of being recognized by men ... [87].

As to the principle sources of international law, he cites in a more positivist vein the writings of the publicists, the opinions of the jurisconsults, diplomatic correspondence, decisions of the prize courts, decisions of international tribunals, decisions of local courts, customs, and treaties and conventions [88].

It is clear that Ribeyro's orientation cannot be designated as anything but eclectic. It is apparent also that his ideas of the persons or subjects of international law are traditional.

MANOEL ALVARO DE SOUZA SÁ VIANNA (1860–1923), a Brazilian writer and diplomat, is perhaps best known for his polemic with Alejandro Alvarez, a matter which will be considered in the following chapter. Sá Vianna, however, contributed in 1908 a general work on international law which has enjoyed a considerable amount of success [89].

International law is based on the natural law, but the two are separate for international law is positive and human law. This conclusion is based on the doctrines of Saint Thomas Aquinas [90]. After recognizing the traditional dualism of natural and positive phases of international law, he adds that this

---

[84] *Ibid.*, pp. 1–2.
[85] *Ibid.*, p. 4.
[86] *Ibid.*, p. 20.
[87] *Ibid.*, p. 21.
[88] *Ibid.*, pp. 11–18.
[89] Manoel Alvarado de Souza Sá Vianna, *Elementos de direito internacional* I (Rio de Janeiro, Jornal do commercio de Rodrigues & co., 1908).
[90] *Ibid.*, pp. 24–25.

dichotomy "... assents in the system of Grotius, it satisfies perfectly the eclectic school, and it is explained under the principle of sociability [91]."

Regarding sources, Sá Vianna, recognizes the two senses in which the word may properly be used, as the "origins from which something proceeds" and as "the documents in which the manifestations of this cause are found."

Regarding the former it is to be observed that natural international law with its source in nature influences greatly the positive international law "... because it is founded on the supreme good and supreme justice ...". Grotius is cited as proof that the natural law "... is the only science which obligates all nations." Tacit or express consent, however, are the sources of the positive international law [92].

As to the second type of source, he notes that the font of natural international law is history, and that international treaties and usages, the national laws of states, court decisions, the writings of the publicists and jurists, and history itself are the sources of positive international law [93].

Perhaps the most succinct statement of legal philosophy in the entire work is the following:

The reason or basis of this law [i.e., international law] is that the human race, although divided into various peoples and dominions, always has some unity, not only specific, but almost political and moral, determined by the natural precept of mutual love and mercy, which is extended to all men, the same to foreigners and regardless of race [94].

Sá Vianna defines international law as "... the complex of rational principles and of rules admitted and accepted voluntarily by states in their direct and indirect reciprocal relations [95]."

Although this remark would seem to indicate that only states are to be considered as persons for purposes of international law, there is some contrary evidence. Much later he observes that all those persons whose situation is regulated by international law ought to be so considered [96].

---

[91] *Ibid.*, p. 72.
[92] *Ibid.*, p. 285.
[93] *Loc. cit.*
[94] *Ibid.*, p. 23.
[95] *Ibid.*, p. 5.
[96] *Ibid.*, p. 300.

"We must recognize", he states, "that in effect the international persons are three — the state, man and the Pope [97]."

Sá Vianna's basic philosophy is best classified as eclecticism. His views as to the persons or subjects of international law are not traditional. It is not clear how far he would go in recognizing individuals as persons of international law, but it is significant that in some degree this recognition is granted.

The two volume work, *Tratado de derecho internacional público*, of D. SIMÓN PLANAS SUÁREZ (1879–   ) published in 1916 is often quoted by Latin American and other writers of international law. This author is a Venezuelan and has written in the fields of international law and relations, and inter-American affairs.

After observing that international law has been variously defined depending upon the school of the person offering the definition, it is suggested that

... in synthesis it is nothing more than the aggregate of rational and positive principles and rules which govern the relations of the states, whether in time of peace or of war [98].

In conformity with the adage, *ubi societas, ibi jus*, Planas Suárez states that international law is grounded on the existence of a community of nations. The binding influence of international law, he intimates, has become progressively stronger [99].

His division of international law is the usual one of natural and positive segments, the former being called theoretical or philosophical. The philosophical segment is made up of the "... principles which the internationalists find more equitable, in relation to an abstract and ideal conception of justice ... [100]." The progress of the philosophical law, moreover, is a factor in the progress of positive law.

As to the positive law, the usual conventional and customary phases thereof are seen as grounded in consent and, in Ribeyro's phrase, in "presumed consent [101]."

After remarking upon the influence of the natural on the positive law, he makes the following observation which is not

[97] *Loc. cit.*
[98] D. Simón Planas Suárez, *Tratado de derecho internacional público* (Madrid, Hijos de Reus, 1916), Vol. I, p. 1.
[99] *Ibid.*, pp. 5–6.
[100] *Ibid.*, p. 13.
[101] *Loc. cit.*

too clear but which seems to suggest something of the way in which the influence is brought to bear.

These rules [of positive law], nevertheless, conform to the principles of *theoretical* law and to the scientific doctrines whenever political situations permit, and they always tend to indicate improvements which, by their reasonable value and intrinsic qualities, have the possibility of forming new elements which, by the will of states, will constitute the source of new principles of *positive* law [102].

This would all seem to indicate that the consent of states is a superficial though essential factor, and that an underlying force is to be seen in the rational or natural principles.

This view is confirmed in the following introductory passage of the work:

We have borne in mind the principal international acts, citing or copying them, because, whatever may be the results of the present historic moment, we believe that the fundamental ideas which inspire them will always live as they are based on principles of justice and of right (*derecho*) [103].

It would appear that Planas Suárez' system is so thoroughly interwoven with both naturalistic and positivistic elements that he cannot be considered as anything but an eclectic. His ideas on the persons or subjects of international law are quite orthodox.

A widely quoted Argentine who wrote for the most part during the first quarter of the twentieth century is EDUARDO L. BIDAU (1862–   ). The 1924 edition of his *Derecho internacional público* has been used in this study [104].

Bidau seems to have been greatly influenced by Amancio Alcorta and he repeats Alcorta's definition that:

International law is the aggregate of rules designed (*destinadas*) to direct the relations among states and to determine the laws and usages applicable to the relations of private law, born under laws and usages of different states [105].

Bidau adds that "Public international law is, consequently, the aggregate of rules designed to direct the relations among states", [106]

---

[102] *Loc. cit.*
[103] *Ibid.*, p. VIII.
[104] Eduardo L. Bidau, *Derecho internacional público* (Buenos Aires, Valerio Abeledo, 1924) 2 vols.
[105] *Ibid.*, Vol. I, pp. 6–7.
[106] *Ibid.*, p. 7.

also that "States are the only subjects or persons of international law [107]."

It may be significant to note that Bidau footnotes the word *"destinados"* (or *"destinées"* in the French edition of Alcorta [108]), translated here as "designed," as follows:

This term indicates that it does not treat of rules which have their origin in the capricious will of men, but [of those] which emanate from the existent law [109].

Bidau employs the usual dichotomy of natural and positive law. The former which he also calls rational law, has to do with the "theoretical laws," while the positive laws are established in such a way as to be binding on states [110].

As to the term *"fuente"* it is correctly observed that it may mean source either in the sense of origin or foundation, or in the sense of evidences (*medios*), of international law [111].

Regarding the foundations the following observation is made:

... the basis of international law is found in principle in the nature common to all men, manifesting itself progressively by the consent of the most civilized peoples [112].

As to evidences (*medios*) of international law, Bidau remarks as follows:

These evidences may be direct or indirect.
The first category corresponds to national law (*derecho nacional*), treaties and usages for the countries which have enacted and applied them, and to the internal laws (*leyes internas*): [*i.e.*,] positive legislation. The indirect evidences are treaties and usages for the countries which have not subscribed to them, diplomatic documents, the opinions of the publicists and writers of international law, economists, philosophers, etc., and lastly the Roman law [113].

It would be arbitrary to categorize Bidau as either a naturalist or a positivist, for he shows ample evidence of both. He follows closely the lead of Alcorta who has been classified elsewhere as

---

[107] *Ibid.*, p. 64.
[108] *Supra*, p. 56.
[109] *Ibid.*, p. 6.
[110] *Ibid.*, p. 7.
[111] *Ibid.*, p. 16.
[112] *Loc. cit.*
[113] *Ibid.*, pp. 16–17.

an eclectic [114], and this designation is the appropriate one for Bidau as well. His views on the persons or subjects of international law are traditional.

The modern Peruvian scholar, ALBERTO ULLOA Y SOTOMAYOR (1894–   ), who is Professor of Public International Law at the University of Lima, is another of the better known contemporary Latin American publicists. The second edition of his *Derecho internacional público* published in 1938 has been used in this survey [115].

After a résumé of the main theories of international law, Ulloa says that

It is now necessary to give to international law a foundation more in accord with the situation which it occupies and with the character of the social evolution begun in the nineteenth century [116].

He suggests that the dominant motivating force in our age is economics and that international law cannot expect to be immune from its influence [117]. Economics does not, however, constitute the whole story. Something else is needed "to ennoble it and facilitate its development." This is the element of morality ". . . which contains the concept of justice and which is expressed by the multiple manifestations of opinion [118]."

Thus the situation is one in which economic forces determine the rule of international law, but nevertheless allow of modification by the moral forces of public opinion [119].

Ulloa's definition of international law, following his perusal of these theories, emerges in his discussion of the economic aspects of international law:

. . . international law is effectively *the result of an equilibrium between the inclination of the preeminently economic interests of the societies which the state represents, develops and defends, and the superior moral sentiments of human fellowship (convivencia) which are expressed through the manifestations of opinion* [120].

---

[114] *Supra*, pp. 57–58.
[115] Alberto Ulloa, *Derecho internacional público* I (Lima, Imprenta Torres Aguirre, 1938).
[116] *Ibid.*, p. 7.
[117] *Loc. cit.*
[118] *Ibid.*, p. 8.
[119] *Loc. cit.*
[120] *Loc. cit.*

Ulloa draws a distinction between foundations (*fundamentos*) and sources (*fuentes*) of international law. In this matter he is far from clear. At one point he observes that the consent of states is:

... not a cause or origin of international rules but a consequence of factors which the state does not control; it is not a foundation of the law but a consequence of the true foundation; [it is merely a] simple formal expression of determinant imperatives [121].

Elsewhere, it is observed that sources (*fuentes*) signify the modes of formation of law, and that, while some writers place the consent of states in this category, to do so confuses the ideas of source and foundation [122].

To add further to the picture, this writer says that he is in complete agreement with the classification of sources in the Statute of the Permanent Court of International Justice (except that he would place the doctrine of the publicists ahead of general principles of justice) [123]. It will be recalled that this classification embodies:

1. General or special international conventions which establish rules recognized expressly by the litigant states;
2. international custom as proof of a practice generally accepted as a juridical norm;
3. the general principles of law recognized by the civilized nations;
4. jurisprudence and the doctrines of the most qualified publicists, as a means to help establish rules of law [124].

Regarding the subjects of international law, Ulloa feels that the traditional view is not appropriate and that in addition to states there are other entities which enjoy international personality. Among these are the Holy See, possibly the League of Nations, and also man himself who "... can be considered as a direct subject of international law ... [125]."

While it may be assumed that parts of Ulloa's thinking are traditionally positivistic, as to the foundations of international law he tends toward economic determinism modified by public opinion as this expresses the concepts of justice and morality.

---

[121] *Ibid.*, p. 14.
[122] *Ibid.*, p. 29.
[123] *Ibid.*, p. 30.
[124] *Ibid.*, pp. 29–30.
[125] *Ibid.*, p. 76.

Ultimately it must be concluded that Ulloa's orientation is similar to that of Duguit, but inclined in the direction of economic determinism. It might be added that in no other writer except Alberdi have economic factors been so highly considered.

Regarding the persons of international law, he adopts the more recent view that the individual as such enjoys international personality.

The orientation of MIGUEL CRUCHAGA TOCORNAL (1869–   ) might suggest that he were more properly considered in the latter section of this chapter which treats of the new international law. His *Derecho internacional*, however, is constructed along the lines of a treatise on international law in general and, consequently, will be considered here.

Cruchaga Tocornal, a Chilean diplomat and academician is one of the better known Latin American writers. His treatise was published in 1944 with a second volume appearing in 1948 [126].

International law and politics are the elements which regulate international relations, and the great questions which divide peoples (now especially economic matters) cannot lend themselves to incorporation into a body of laws [127].

Although of the opinion that international law must be modernized, he observes that such modernization would not constitute a new international law in as much as "The fundamental principles are always essentially the same and rest on the immutable foundations of justice and morality [128]."

A distinction is drawn between the positive law (*ley* or *derecho positivo*) and right (*derecho*). The former consists of laws made by society to keep order and otherwise to facilitate relationships and which can and should be changed from time to time. Right (*derecho*), on the other hand, is "... on a superior plane. It is the source of the positive laws [129]." The positive laws change but right (*derecho*) will last as long as the civilization which created it, and it will inspire the various laws which society dictates [130].

---

[126] Miguel Cruchaga Tocornal, *Derecho internacional* (Santiago, Chile, Editorial nascimento, 1944–8) 2 vols.
[127] *Ibid.*, Vol. I, p. 5.
[128] *Ibid.*, p. 7.
[129] *Loc. cit.*
[130] *Loc. cit.*

After a discussion of the various theories of international law, Cruchaga Tocornal concludes that "The diverse schools show that international law recognizes *morality* and *natural law* as its basis [131]."

Thus, states, like individuals, are linked together by rights and duties "... which emanate from their very nature and which each civilization has recognized as *principles of natural law* ... [132]." Both internal laws and treaties should be imbued with the idea of natural law [133].

As to sources of international law, he indicates customs, treaties, international court decisions, national laws, such documents as protocols and manifestos (*i.e.*, "books of color"), acts of scientific institutions, state records, and the works of the publicists [134]. Of these the first two are preeminent [135].

Cruchaga observes, in a way which shows the influence of such writers as Duguit, Spiropolous, and Alvarez, that public opinion is a strong factor in making law obligatory.

International law is a positive law in the strict sense of the word, because it unites the characteristics which are necessary for it to exist: the *conviction* of the people that there is a body of law which contains *obligatory precepts* [136].

This is amplified by the view — also from Alvarez — that international law is not basically juridical, but rather psychological and political [137].

Regarding definitions, Cruchaga Tocornal lists the views of nine writers, himself concluding that "... public international law would be the aggregate of principles and rules which govern the mutual juridical relations of states [138]."

Among the entities enjoying international personality, are listed states, mandates, belligerent communities, the League of Nations, the Permanent Court of International Justice, the International Labor Organization, and numerous bureaus like

---

[131] *Ibid.*, p. 206.
[132] *Loc. cit.*
[133] *Ibid.*, pp. 206–207.
[134] *Ibid.*, pp. 251–255.
[135] *Ibid.*, p. 251.
[136] *Ibid.*, pp. 190–191.
[137] *Ibid.*, p. 191 *et passim*. This matter will be taken up in detail later in this chapter in connection with the work of Alejandro Alvarez.
[138] *Ibid.*, p. 188.

the Universal Postal Union [139]. In addition Cruchaga Tocornal speaks at length about the alleged international personality of the individual observing that a trend toward such recognition exists. He concludes, however, against the view that the individual enjoys personality in this sense, and offers as proof that the individual cannot hail a state into an international court [140].

In speaking of persons of international law, it is suggested that "States are the true members of the 'international community' called *Magna Civitas* [141]"; also the general tenor is that states enjoy a distinctly superior position.

In a section of Volume II, written some years later, this slight modification of his earlier view is advanced:

In summary, the individual as a human person, and by his condition as such is the subject of certain faculties which are his own and which, on being invocable under any sovereignty, are extended to the field of international law. But we believe that the state, a natural moral person and therefore titulary of rights and obligations, is the subject par excellence of international law [142].

It is safe to conclude that Cruchaga Tocornal is an eclectic who is imbued with some aspects of sociological jurisprudence. His view regarding international persons is only slightly removed from the traditional position, but it must be acknowledged that to some slight degree he does recognize the individual as a subject of international law.

One of the best known and most widely quoted of contemporary Latin American writers of international law is HILDEBRANDO POMPEO PINTO ACCIOLY (1888–   ), a Brazilian who has taught and written widely in the field of international law, who was a Brazilian delegate to the League of Nations, and who has been with the Brazilian foreign service in many capacities.

His principal treatise on international law was originally published in Portuguese and has been translated into French and Spanish editions. The Spanish edition, *Tratado de derecho internacional público* published in 1945 and 1946, has been the basis of the present notice [143].

---

[139] *Ibid.*, pp. 303–305.
[140] *Ibid.*, pp. 308–309.
[141] *Ibid.*, p. 304.
[142] *Ibid.*, Vol. II, p. 402.
[143] Hildebrando Accioly, *Tratado de derecho internacional publico* (Rio de Janeiro, Imprensa nacional, 1945–6) 3 vols.

Accioly defines international law as

... the aggregate of rules or principles designed (*destinados*) to regulate the international rights and duties not only of states and other analgous organisms endowed with such rights and duties, but also of individuals [144].

While he does not agree with Duguit that individuals are the only persons of international law, and though he emphasizes that states are persons in international law [145], he is emphatic in his stand that individuals have international personality as well.

After a short discussion of the persons of international law he concludes as follows:

In summary, international public law considers as persons: the state, certain collectivities [*e.g.*, the League of Nations] and man taken individually. Without doubt the state is still the most important, but one cannot deny the inclusion of the rest in the category of international persons, at least from certain points of view [146].

Much more is said in this vein but the above is the crux of the matter [147].

Regarding the basis of international law, Accioly reviews the major theories, the last of which is the "new doctrine of natural law." This, he carefully points out, is not the seventeenth century conception of inalienable rights which allegedly existed prior to the advent of civil society, but rather the result of the observation of facts. He quotes Le Fur as follows:

... law is not a simple formula, the expression of the arbitrary will of the state; it has an end, a tenor which is its essence and it is summarized in the notion of the common good, the good of the group, [whether] national or world, which is destined to rule. In law ... two necessary elements must be distinguished; the foundation (*fondo*) and the form. The principles which constitute the foundation are, moreover, very restricted and are reduced to two basic rules, which are a direct application of the notion of justice. These two rules are: the obligation to maintain contracted promises and the duty to repair damages caused unjustly ... [148].

---

[144] *Ibid.*, Vol. I, p. 2.
[145] *Ibid.*, p. 83.
[146] *Ibid.*, p. 87.
[147] *Ibid.*, pp. 495–644 *et passim*.
[148] *Ibid.*, p. 13.

A little later on Accioly observes that "... the true basis of international law is the natural law, such as it is now conceived [149]." The basis of the obligatory character of international law is "the juridical conscience of man."

International law is valid because men have conscience, [and] are convinced of its validity, that is, of the obligatory character of its rules [150].

As to the sources of international law, Accioly mentions three: the general principles of law, customs, and treaties and conventions [151].

Of these, the first is the true and basic one and serves both as the basis for the rest and as a means of interpreting the positive rules. The latter two are the two great sources of positive international law [152].

The principles of law are norms of objective justice on which pure law is based. They are principles of superior order, and exist in the juridical conscience of men. They obtain whether they are recognized as internal law or not, since recognition is merely additional proof of their existence [153].

What has been said is ample to establish Accioly's status as the most naturalistic of the Latin American eclectics of this century, and as a follower of Le Fur. He occupies a position which reflects the restive tenor of the times and shows the influence also of Krabbe and Duguit whom he often cites. With respect to the subjects of international law, he includes in this category not only the traditional ones but also man as an individual.

The Argentine, Luis A. Podestá Costa (1885–   ), is an outstanding contemporary Latin American writer on international law. The second edition of his work, *Manual de derecho internacional público*, published in 1947, was used in this study [154].

The two main sources of international law, he says, are custom and treaties which, because they proceed from the organs which

---

[149] *Ibid.*, p. 14.
[150] *Loc. cit.*
[151] *Ibid.*, p. 21.
[152] *Ibid.*, p. 22.
[153] *Loc. cit.*
[154] L. A. Podestá Costa, *Manual de derecho internacional publico* (Buenos Aires, Artes graficas Bartolome U. Chiesino, 1947).

manage international relations, are called direct [155]. Among lesser sources are the general principles of law, jurisprudence of either national or international origin (*i.e.*, court decisions), the doctrines of qualified writers and of scientific institutions, and domestic laws when these relate to international law [156]. There is a third category also regarded as a source, though of still less significance. This consists of the non-binding but morally persuasive recommendations, declarations, *etc.* of such groups as the League of Nations, the Organization of the United Nations, and the Pan American Union [157].

Regarding methodology, Podestá Costa states that neither the historical nor the deductive method by itself is a satisfactory basis for the understanding of international law. The former tends to legalize abuses of force and confuses law and fact; while the latter leads to inflexible and rigid rules which are not scientifically established. The historical method and the "deductive-inductive method," therefore, should be combined into what Podestá Costa calls the eclectic method such as will lead to a "... reasoned analysis and permit a balanced and just solution to be found [158]."

After a brief résumé of a few systems of international law such as those of Grotius, Jellinek, and Kelsen, he observes that the new idea of natural law (*i.e.*, the view held by Le Fur and others) is nearer to reality. "This theory", he says,

does not now sustain the existence of a natural law of man, anterior to life in society and of an immutable and inalienable character; it establishes that the principles of international law are reduced to two fundamental norms, which are a direct application of the notion of justice: the obligation of fulfilling contracted promises and the duty of repairing damages caused unjustly. From this it results that the principle *pacta sunt servanda* constitutes one of the bases of the newest conception of natural law; but, above this principle, reigns the idea of justice, which is asserted to in the juridical conscience of men, and this notion is that which gives obligatory character to its norms [159].

[155] *Ibid.*, p. 14.
[156] *Ibid.*, p. 15.
[157] *Ibid.*, pp. 15–16.
[158] *Ibid.*, p. 28.
[159] *Ibid.*, p. 29.

By way of definition, he says that

International public law is constituted as (*por*) the aggregate of norms which govern the relations of the states among themselves and also of these [*i.e.*, states] with certain entities which, although not states, possess international personality [160].

The entities which enjoy international personality are states, the Holy See, some British dominions, a number of semi-states like Byelorussia and the Ukraine, and certain aggregates of states such as the League of Nations and the Organization of the United Nations. These enjoy legal personality on the international level by virtue of the fact that states have allowed them to obtain that status [161]. The individual, however, has no international personality [162].

It must be concluded that while Podestá Costa shows some preference for positive sources of international law, his predilections regarding fundamental sources are in the direction of a modern form of natural law. All in all it is apparent that this author is of an eclectic disposition. As to the persons or subjects of international law, he is essentially traditional.

Part II

THE NEW INTERNATIONAL LAW

The concept of the new international law represents, as has often been said before [163], an attempt to break down the vicious character of the present international order. The partisans in this movement have been largely of a monist persuasion, and have not been averse, on the whole, to the espousal of relatively drastic innovations.

The Latin American counterpart of this world wide movement is no less remarkable or virile than are its segments in other parts of the world. While there seems to be little organic relationship among the ideas of the various writers who are noticed in the present work, two show the influence of Duguit, one of these same writers shows also the imprint of Le Fur, a third evidences the mark of Kelsen, and two others, of less theoretical

---

[160] *Ibid.*, p. 13.
[161] *Ibid.*, pp. 32–35.
[162] *Ibid.*, p. 33.
[163] *Supra*, pp. 33–37.

bent, follow a unique thesis which might be labeled the Brazilian conception of the new international law.

It may be safely asserted that all of the writers reviewed here show remarkable originality and have made significant contributions to the theory of international law.

Of all the Latin American publicists past or present the most prolific writer by far is the Chilean member of the World Court, ALEJANDRO O. ALVAREZ (1868–   ). His literary productions have spanned the past half century, and he has been active in numerous international associations and has been a delegate to many international conferences.

Alvarez is probably best known for his thesis that there exists a characteristically American international law, a matter which will be surveyed in the following chapter. There are certain aspects of his writings, however, which relate to the philosophy of international law in general, and it is with these matters that this section is concerned [164].

Alvarez observes that legal philosophy has gone through several periods. These are the "... metaphysical in antiquity; theological in the middle age; rationalistic in its form of natural law in the seventeenth and eighteenth centuries [165]." As to the nineteenth century, legal philosophy varied with the method of study employed, *i.e.*, the historical, sociological, materialistic, and idealistic approaches each entailed its own methodology [166].

The French revolution inaugurated a social and legal regime stressing individualism, which became, and for a time remained, the central theme and the basic ethos of social phenomena. Since the middle of the nineteenth century, however, Alvarez, like many others, would stress that a break-down in individualism has been under way and that in its place a form of cooperation has been taking root. This mutuality is the theme of the present epoch [167].

---

[164] Alvarez' works are often cumulative in that the later works include most of what has been mentioned in earlier studies. For this reason, some of the more recent works have been used rather extensively here for purposes of documentation. The later works also are often clearer than their predecessors. The reader will find a fairly extensive list of Alvarez' books and articles in the bibliography.

[165] Alejandro Alvarez, 'New Conception and New Bases of Legal Philosophy' *Illinois Law Review*, Vol. XIII, (1918–9) p. 171.

[166] *Loc. cit.*

[167] Alejandro Alvarez, 'La futura sociedad de las naciones' *Actas memorias y*

Since the social ethos has changed, the basis of law must also change; the central theme of international law must become that of interdependence rather than of the earlier individualistic conception of state sovereignty [168].

In order to restore the respect which international law has lost as a result of its unrealistic orientation toward individualism, Alvarez suggests that it must be studied in a new fashion. This study "... must be *synthetic* and must examine the life of peoples, in their full *extent* and in all their *profundity* [169]." This means that the important influences on international life must be emphasized and that these influences must be understood in terms of the epochs in which they occurred. With the term "profundity" Alvarez means to urge the consideration of all material (*i.e.*, pertaining to the social milieu) and immaterial (*i.e.*, psychological) factors, rather than merely the narrowly legalistic aspects which have been regarded heretofore [170].

This entails the creation of two "new" sciences which are termed studies of *International Life* and of the *Psychology of Peoples in International Matters* [171]. These involve, respectively, studies of international law as it was and is affected by all international phenomena [172], and of psychological attitudes including such elements as confidence, cooperation, hatred, desires for revenge, *i.e.*, in general, notions of sociability and antisociability [173].

This all leads directly to a central element in Alvarez' thought, namely, his conception of international law (as well as of national public law) as being not a strictly juridical science, but rather, a social science — a psychological and political discipline [174]. International law is an "essentially *political social* and *psychological*" law rather than a strictly juridical force like national private law. Furthermore, it has neither legislator nor sanction; never-

proyectos de las sesiones de La Habana; *Instituto americano de derecho internacional*, (1918), p. 246.

[168] Alejandro Alvarez, 'Introduccion' to Miguel Cruchaga Tocornal, *op. cit.*, pp. XX–XXV.

[169] Alejandro Alvarez, *Despues de la guerra* (Buenos Aires, Imprenta de la Universidad, 1943) p. 123.

[170] *Ibid.*, pp. 123–124. Also Alvarez, 'Introduccion' p. XXII.

[171] Alvarez, *Despues de la guerra*, p. 127.

[172] *Ibid.*, p. 310.

[173] *Ibid.*, p. 195.

[174] *Ibid.*, p. 419.

theless, it is binding and therefore it is considered by Alvarez to be positive law [175].

In this vein Alvarez carefully observes that his collegue, Louis Le Fur, was not sufficiently precise, when, in outlining the former's views, Le Fur attributed to Alvarez the thought that international law "took into consideration" politics and psychology [176]. Says Alvarez:

This is not exactly my opinion. What I maintain is that international law *not only takes into account* politics and the psychology of peoples but that it has essentially these qualities (*characteres*). Furthermore, and completing my ideas in this respect, I will say that said elements, united to the exigencies of social life, *form or constitute* this law; from these it is born spontaneously and directly [177].

By way of further explanation of his view of the relation of these elements to international law, he draws a contrast with national law:

National law, especially social legislation, *is inspired by or takes into account* these factors, but they do not by themselves form this legislation.

In international law the said elements incorporate themselves into it, they are what constitute it; one does not treat then of a legislator who takes them into account. The best proof of my affirmation is that, if these factors are modified, by that circumstance alone the law appears antiquated in this connection (*su conjunto*) or in the matter expressly affected by the change, and it is not respected [178].

While it is true that principles of private law have been taken over by international law and are adhered to, nevertheless, in these instances "... the principles correspond to the exigencies of life and thus take on a psychological and social quality [179]."

The political aspect is presumably clear enough to be dropped at this point. Of the psychological element, however, it might be observed that ideas of interdependence, fundamental rights, vital interests, and the like, are psychological or mental or intellectual concepts that depend largely upon the attitudes

[175] *Ibid.*, pp. 286–287.
[176] *Ibid.*, pp. 287–288.
[177] *Ibid.*, p. 288.
[178] *Loc. cit.*
[179] *Ibid.*, p. 289.

which prevail regarding them [180]. In 1934 Alvarez had expressed the intimately related view that the public conscience is the source from which the great principles of international law are for the most part derived [181]. This, however, may not be an exact account of his later view; for in another work it is suggested that the sources of international law are customs, conventions, and the juridical conscience together with principles drawn from national law and court decisions, and the spontaneous development of precepts [182]. According to this same work, the sanction which international law now enjoys is that of public opinion [183]. All in all, it is apparent that these writings, as a whole, are geared to the identical conception, namely, that of the psychological nature of international law.

As a result of this politico-psychological character of international law, and of the relation of social interdependency in general to this conception, a number of innovations have come into being, in Alvarez' view, two of which must be mentioned here.

The first, having to do with the relationship between international law and national law, sees national sovereignty as a concept which is becoming progressively more limited. Though it has not and will not entirely disappear, its claim to absoluteness is now restrained [184].

The second of these innovations is concerned with the matter of what entities enjoy international personality. Since the middle of the nineteenth century when states and the Papacy were the only subjects of international law, the scope of international personality has widened to include continents, groups of states, peoples, minorities, international associations, and

---

[180] *Ibid.*, pp. 291–294.
[181] Alejandro Alvarez, 'Les sources du droit des gens' *Annuaire de l'institut de droit international* (Octobre, 1934) p. 498. See also Alejandro Alvarez, 'De la necessidad de una nueva concepcion del derecho' *Anales de la Universidad.* Republica de Chile, (1930), p. 196.
[182] Alvarez, 'Introduccion,' p. XXXI.
[183] *Ibid.*, p. XXXII.
[184] *Ibid.*, pp. XXXIV–XXXV; also *ibid.*, p. LXXIII (this last is in the 'Declaration sur les donnes fondamentales et les grands principes du droit international moderne' which Alvarez includes at this point and which has been approved by several scientific associations). See also Alvarez, *Despues de la guerra*, pp. 285, 425–427.

the individual himself [185]. In all these cases this personality, though often to be qualified, is seen in some measure to exist.

Alvarez' name has often been connected with proposals of codification of international law [186], but his more recent remarks on the matter have suggested that the unsettled conditions of the world (1944) would seem to indicate the desirability of a temporary suspension of this work. It is further observed that when codification is utilized it should apply only to the law of such matters as involve important difficulties, and even then it should be neither detailed nor exhaustive lest it fail to allow the exigencies of international life to work matters out in conformity with reality [187].

Although Alvarez is often repetitious, frequently ambiguous and not sufficiently explanative, yet it is clear that he is within the tradition of the new international law and that he has made a distinct and valuable contribution to the law of nations. He sees international law, as do the sociological jurists, in terms of social phenomena, and like Spiropolous, he stresses the psychological aspects involved in the notion of juridical consciousness. Alvarez is unique in that he conceives of international politics and psychology as of the essence of international law rather than as factors which this takes into consideration. The state is seen as being limited by and subordinate to international law. Moreover, the individual is included as a subject of the law of nations.

One of the most interesting of the Latin American works advocating the new international law is that of the Colombian, EDGARDO MANOTAS WILCHES. This work, first appearing in Spanish in 1946, was translated into French and published in 1948 with a somewhat critical preface by Georges Scelle [188].

The introduction and the first part of the book deal with the subject of monism vs. dualism, and with the history of the theory of international law. In these sections the author shows

[185] Alvarez, *Despues de la guerra*, pp. 284–285; also Alvarez, 'Introduccion,' pp. XXX–XXXI.

[186] See especially Alexandre Alvarez, *La codification du droit international* (Paris, A. Pedone, 1912), and Alejandro Alvarez, *La codificacion del derecho internacional en America* (Santiago de Chile, Imprenta universitaria, 1923).

[187] Alvarez, 'Introduccion,' pp. LXIV–LXVI.

[188] Edgardo Manotas Wilches, *Le nouveau droit des gens* (Paris, Librairie du recueil sirey, 1948).

a preference for monism [189], and for a merging of the idea of social solidarity with the new concept of natural law [190].

What Manotas Wilches attempts to do in the body of his work is to reconcile natural law and social solidarity. He feels that there is little real difference between the ideas of Duguit and Scelle on the one hand, and those of the naturalists on the other, as both of these views are founded on the Aristotelian conception of the social man [191].

An attempt is made to establish the social nature of man on a completely scientific and irrefutable basis. This is done by reference to the studies of the psychologist, Alfred Adler, who "... lays down as the basis of his system this *absolute verity* that social life is the normal and natural form of our existence [192]."

Man is so helpless, as an isolated individual, that close community relationship is an absolute necessity [193], and, "In a word the school of Adler shows experimentally that the laws of solidarity and of social cooperation are inherent in human nature [194]." Social solidarity supplies the basis for determining justice and injustice. "All that which is harmonized with human solidarity is just, all that which contradicts it is unjust [195]." Perhaps Manotas Wilches' meaning and orientation is best clarified in the following remark:

Humanity in the different epochs of its development has shown the absolute truth which is social solidarity. From the sociological point of view, religions are nothing but the great movements of human solidarity, of which the highest expression is found in Christianity. The God of the Christians and his only son, Jesus, brother of men, unifies us under the sign of a paternal community. The commandment to love your neighbor is nothing but the religious translation of the sentiment of social solidarity [196].

The third part of the book is devoted to the primacy of international law in the monist system, and the position of the individual under international law.

---

[189] *Ibid.*, pp. 2–4.
[190] *Ibid.*, pp. 16–22.
[191] *Ibid.*, pp. 23–24.
[192] *Ibid.*, p. 30.
[193] *Ibid.*, pp. 33–34.
[194] *Ibid.*, p. 142.
[195] *Ibid.*, p. 59.
[196] *Ibid.*, p. 46.

It is felt that sovereignty is not a quality which the state enjoys in its own right, but rather "... a competency conferred by the law of nations [197]." Sovereignty and independence are synonomous. "A state is sovereign because it is independent of all the others, but all have submitted to the sovereignty of international law [198]."

Manotas Wilches observes that like Kelsen, he too subscribes to a hierarchy of norms, but while Kelsen's view rests on the basis of a "dialectical superposition," his own system employs a hierarchy founded on collective life. It begins with the individual and "... is successively spread up to its summit on the waves of social solidarity [199]." Consequently, once the mask of national sovereignty has been shattered, two facts pertaining to international personality are apparent, namely that "... individuals are the natural subjects of international law," and that states are also subjects of the law of nations [200].

Although natural law and the religious aspects of this conception already have been mentioned, it should be particularly emphasized that solidarity is viewed as a basically natural phenomenon. "I ought to add ...", he says,

that this necessity [*i.e.*, the necessity of guaranteeing inter-social cooperation] is merged, it is identified, with the belief in the natural law of nations conceived as the conjunction of these absolute objective values: justice and equity [201].

In summary it can be noted that Manotas Wilches' system of a new international law tries to ground social solidarity on a scientific basis and thus to merge it with natural law. He recognizes the individual and the state as persons under international law and sees national sovereignty as limited by the law of nations.

There is considerable indication that the Pure Theory of Law has been an important factor in certain phases of Latin American legal philosophy [202], but evidence of its im-

[197] *Ibid.*, p. 76.
[198] *Loc. cit.*
[199] *Ibid.*, p. 82.
[200] *Ibid.*, p. 83.
[201] *Ibid.*, p. 136.
[202] Josef L. Kunz, *Latin-American Philosophy of Law in the Twentieth Century* (New York, New York University School of Law, 1950). Also, Luis Recasens Siches, Carlos Cosio, Juan Llamabias de Azevedo, Eduardo Garcia Maynez, *Latin-American Legal Philosophy* (Cambridge, Harvard University Press, 1948).

pression on writers primarily interested in international law has not yet become too apparent.

An interesting exception, however, is the little work of the Brazilian, PEDRO BAPTISTA MARTINS, (1896–1951), which was first published in 1933 and again, with no alteration, in 1942 [203].

The greater part of this work is devoted to sketches of the various theories of international law together with reasons for their inacceptability. In the later part of his study, however, Martins builds an interesting case for Kelsen's view.

The hierarchy of norms characteristic of the Pure Theory of Law has often encountered difficulty in explaining to the satisfaction of skeptics the apparent inconsistency between the view on the one hand that international law is superior to national law, and on the other hand the dualist-incorporationist thesis which nearly always seems to express actual international practice. This dilemma Martins resolves by pointing out that the League of Nations, as a going concern, symbolizes the sphere of the higher norms which delimit the area of state action [204].

The economic and even military sanctions of the League are pointed to as the means by which enforcement can be exacted [205]. The fact that these measures may not always be successful is disposed of with the remark that:

Those who understand that the existence of war implies the juridical negation of internationalism are restrained, by a duty of coherence, to maintain that the existence of crime is the negation of penal law [206].

Pacta sunt servanda, derived from custom, is considered to be the basis of all law; at the same time the sociological, economic and ethical factors are elements which, though in themselves outside the scope of law, are expressed through custom, and which, in the last analysis through their recognition in the juridical conscience, validate customs, hence *pacta sunt servanda*, and ultimately all law [207].

Paraphrasing Kelsen himself, it can be affirmed that it is not

[203] Pedro Baptista Martins, *Da unidade do direito e da supremacia de direito internacional* (Rio de Janeiro, Imprensa nacional, 1942), p. 5.
[204] *Ibid.*, pp. 73–74.
[205] *Ibid.*, p. 79.
[206] *Ibid.*, p. 80.
[207] *Ibid.*, pp. 76–78.

properly in juridical custom, but in its mental representation, that the normative authority resides, the generative force of law [208].

In summary, it may be noted that while there seems to be no interest shown here in the international personality of the individual, Martins expresses an interesting practical application of the Pure Theory of Law to recent — and, in fact, contemporary — world society.

Very few Latin American works on international law have been translated into English, but one of the rare exceptions is the little book by JORGE AMERICANO (1891–   ) entitled *The New Foundation of International Law* [209]. Americano is a Brazilian scholar who has written considerably regarding legal matters as well as about the University of São Paulo where he is Professor of Law and, where for a time, he served as president.

"Law", he says, "is a system of guarantees based on principles of justice [210]", yet international law at present is not justly ordered, and what must be done is to reform the foundations in such a way that it will be based on justice [211].

In renovating the system of international law, Americano wants to employ the Four Freedoms (freedom from fear and want and of speech and worship) as a bill of rights under international law. He states that the Four Freedoms became international law by virtue of the Atlantic Charter and, in fact, that the chief object of the law of nations is to guarantee these freedoms [212].

Among the many ideas designed to implement these Four Freedoms which are suggested in this work are the following two of considerable interest. Persons under international law will necessarily include the superstate, natural persons, nations, groups or leagues of nations, and international autarchies (*e.g.*, UNNRA) [213]; and, secondly, the state must be limited by the international order [214]. This last includes the stipulation that

---

[208] *Ibid.*, p. 78.
[209] Jorge Americano, *The New Foundation of International Law* (New York, The Macmillan Company, 1947).
[210] *Ibid.*, p. IX.
[211] *Ibid.*, p. X.
[212] *Ibid.*, p. 5.
[213] *Ibid.*, p. 7.
[214] *Ibid.*, pp. 26–27.

there shall be required of each state an effective bill of rights
for the protection of international persons, the submission to
the decisions of the International Court of Justice and to the
laws of the international legislature, the "non-identification of
state and party", the "proportional representation of minorities",
the derivation of its legislative and executive powers from the
ballot, and the "duty to cooperate with the superstate [215]."

The organization of this rather remarkable system calls for a
fairly strong executive branch to exercise police power, to ad-
minister the activities of the superstate, and to assure the enforcement of assembly and court decisions [216]; a judicial system
which would consist of a supreme court and apparently would
be much like the present International Court of Justice except
that it would have compulsory jurisdiction [217]; and a legislative
branch consisting of one chamber in which states and literate
voting populations would be represented. In addition, "The international autarchies should constitute consultative bodies of the
International Assembly [218]."

Voting procedure in the international legislature would consist of two ballotings, the first of which would register only the
votes of the nation states on the basis of one vote for each. On
the second ballot the various national groups which had been
represented in the national elections of each country could register a number of votes equal to their assumed proportion of the
literate population [219]. This would be computed in the following
fashion:

... in a republic with a literate population of twenty million,
four million voted and elected a president by a majority of
two million. This means that three-fourths of the electorate,
corresponding to three-fourths of the population, has not only
elected the government to rule the nation but given it an international mandate to represent fifteen million of the citizens.
The other five million will have representatives elected by the re-
spective parties, proportionate in number to the votes they
polled.

By this system the people of a nation may have one, two

[215] *Ibid.*, p. 27.
[216] *Ibid.*, p. 66.
[217] *Ibid.*, p. 75.
[218] *Ibid.*, pp. 61–62.
[219] *Ibid.*, pp. 63–65.

or more representatives, the total of whose votes correspond to the total literate population, fractions being ignored [220].

If the results of both ballots were the same the resolution or other act would pass, but if no such agreement obtained "redemocratization" would be in order. Although this "redemocratization" process is not described, Americano indicates that the international body would have the right to institute new elections if it were of the opinion that minorities were not properly represented, and it may be assumed that that is what he has in mind regarding "redemocratization [221]."

In order to carry out the entire system envisioned by Americano, it would be necessary to set up an educational program of a sort which would support the plan. "What will be the use", he says,

of organizing an international community to secure minimum rights for free men if education is allowed to take the lines of a philosophy to breed hatred among nations and destroy those rights [222]?

The educational system which he outlines would call for such elements as a manual arts program to accomplish vocational training and to foster hobbies in order to give each person a means to work off excess energy [223]; and a concerted effort to gear the teaching of the social sciences to the defense, glorification, and maintenance of peace [224]. In summary of the educational functions, he mentions three purposes. 1. "As a means of fighting repressions that lead to war." This includes hobbies, crafts, art, music, sports, *etc.* 2. "As a means of fortifying men in democratic convictions." This includes emphasis on the nature of democracy, the need for equality, *etc.* and 3. "As a means of giving confidence in regard to international action." This includes teaching the idea that the international community is organized so as to secure the desired values and that it can be effective only when it has the backing of all people and of all countries [225].

The general idea of this proposal is succinctly put in this

[220] *Ibid.*, p. 62.
[221] *Ibid.*, pp. 62–63.
[222] *Ibid.*, p. 84.
[223] *Ibid.*, pp. 91–92.
[224] *Ibid.*, pp. 93–99.
[225] *Ibid.*, pp. 136–137.

short passage taken from the Foreward to the American edition:

But as a matter of fact the ground has been prepared, and the decision rests with a few hundred persons all over the world — the professors of international law.

If — instead of basing their instruction on an over-emphasized sovereignty, on the old concepts of war as a relation to be stated under "rules of war," on neutrality toward belligerents as a duty for all nations—they would teach that morals should be the same under both domestic and international law, that war is a crime, that there should be a world organization with powers of control and coercion, based on democratic principles, and capable of applying a Bill of Rights to men all over the world, then the few hundred professors of international law could do the greatest work ever done. Every year some thousands of students would assimilate those ideas, and within a few years a strong international consciousness would be formed.

These students would become politicians, journalists, diplomats, economists, professors, educators, and the face of the world would be changed [226].

The approach represents an admission of the basic character of public opinion in any legal system. Americano's plan would attempt to achieve peace by means of a democratic superstate in which the individual is recognized as having international personality. The objectives of the plan are to be supported — and presumably instituted — by appropriate education.

While this system has a certain logic, nevertheless, in the present writer's opinion, it contains an element of naïvete. The passage quoted above, having to do with the ability of the professors of international law to change the world [227], assumes the questionable point that students fairly hang on their instructors' words; also the system of assuring minority representation [228], while embodying a desirable ideal, is set forth with apparently no thought for political considerations such, for example, as have emasculated a portion of the second section of the fourteenth amendment to the Constitution of the United States.

In the last analysis, however, it must be said that Americano comes to grips with some of the most perplexing problems of contemporary world society, and, the fact that he outlines a

[226] *Ibid.*, p. VI.
[227] *Loc. cit.*
[228] *Supra*, pp. 114–115.

very original and to a degree plausible plan for the implementation of basic rights regarded as new developments of actual international law constitutes a contribution not without interest.

Another Brazilian scholar who expresses views quite similar to those of his compatriot, Jorge Americano, is ILMAR PENNA MARINHO (1913–   ), a relatively young foreign service officer and writer on legal subjects.

Although of the opinion that states must be equally respected [229] and although opposed to the unanimity principle, Marinho's conception of equality has nothing of the ring of national sovereignty about it [230].

Virtually the central theme in this work is an advocacy of the notion of interdependence.

In a word: the new juridical order is to be based fundamentally on the policy of absolute interdependence and strict international collaboration [231].

Marinho goes much further than merely to advise collaboration, however, for he suggests that there are certain rules and principles which the states must submit to and must incorporate into their own constitutional systems. His point of view resembles closely that of Americano, this being especially true of such notions as those of submission to the International Court of Justice, acceptance of a necessary limitation on sovereignty, assurance that the Four Freedoms of the Atlantic Charter will be respected, cooperation to enforce peace, and the establishment of democratic bases for government [232].

To these ends Marinho advocates strong collective security with a form of international police [233], and he supports the Baruch plan of atomic control [234]. The idea of neutrality is completely repudiated [235], and, with reference to the problem of legislative representation in the international organization, Americano's proportional arrangement is approved [236].

---

[229] Ilmar Penna Marinho, *Caracteristicas essencias do novo direito internacional* (Rio de Janeiro, Imprensa nacional, 1947).
[230] *Ibid.*, pp. 104–105.
[231] *Ibid.*, p. 21.
[232] *Ibid.*, pp. 41–42.
[233] *Ibid.*, p. 138.
[234] *Ibid.*, p. c. 138.
[235] *Ibid.*, pp. 173–178.
[236] *Ibid.*, p. 108.

As in most of the systems of what is envisaged as the new international law, the plan outlined here calls for recognition of the individual as a person under international law.

Examining the problem with the required attention, we arrive at the conclusion that, although many authors deny it, there exist, in fact, besides states, other international persons, among which the individual is numbered [237].

The thought here is closely related to Marinho's view of the Atlantic Charter which, along with the Declaration of the United Nations, proclaim the Four Freedoms as essential principles of the new international law. This has the effect of elevating the individual to the position of the "primordial subject of international law [238]."

Marinho recognizes, as does Americano, the necessity for a general sentiment which will approve and support the new conception of international law. Note is made of Krabbe's emphasis on the spiritual force upon which the whole vitality of law is based [239]. The place which education must play in the new system is emphasized. Education, it is urged, should be employed to teach a sentiment for democracy, justice, and peace:

It will be an efficacious instrument in the maintenance of peace and security in the world and... it will be inserted among those elements capable of turning international law into that which, until now, it has not succeeded in being — the supreme law of Humanity [240].

This work, as has been said, follows the earlier one of Americano [241]. It emphasizes interdependence, limitation of sovereignty, the international personality of the individual, the importance of the Atlantic Charter, and the place of education in achieving all of these objectives.

There are, of course, other Latin American writers whose works are within the general tradition of the new international law. A few of these have been surveyed, yet no attempt will be made here to detail the general content of these. It is significant, however, that of the reformist writers, most are of

---

[237] *Ibid.*, p. 181.
[238] *Ibid.*, p. 189.
[239] *Ibid.*, p. 72.
[240] *Ibid.*, p. 75.
[241] The Brazilian edition of Americano's work appeared about 1945.

the opinion that the individual should be considered as a subject of international law [242]. Also, the much emphasized ideas of social solidarity or interdependence [243], and of the limitation of national sovereignty [244], are among the points strongly supported by these writers. It is of much significance that this support has been, in fact, widespread.

Conclusions

On the basis of the evidence presented in Chapter III, the following conclusions can be drawn:

1. The eclecticism which encompassed the entire nineteenth century as far as the Latin American publicists were concerned was little or no less in evidence in the twentieth century. Almost all of the writers reviewed displayed at least some elements of it.

2. Traditional positivism, though criticized, has remained a strong element throughout the first half of the twentieth century. This is reflected not only in the ten works labeled as such, but also in the fact that naturalism appeared only in an eclectic form in the representative works reviewed in Part I.

3. Naturalism, as was suggested above, appeared only in an eclectic form, although in a few cases the relative emphasis on natural law was fairly high. While all of the works were eclectic to a degree, only eight of the eighteen reviewed in Part I were thought to contain a sufficient amount of the naturalistic element to merit the designation of eclectic in the classificational sense in which it has been employed here.

4. Of the eighteen writers reviewed in Part I, seven showed at least some recognition of the individual as an international

---

[242] Levi Carneiro, *O direito internacional e a democracia* (Rio de Janeiro, A. Coelho Branco, 1945) pp. 46, 109, 126. Also César Díaz Cisneros, *Estudios de derecho internacional publico* (La Plata, Est. Tip. 'Alberdi', M. Sciocco y cia., 1926) p. 27. Also José María Velasco Ibarra, *Derecho internacional del futuro* (Buenos Aires, Editorial Americalee, 1943) pp. 61–67, 121–126. Eduardo Jimenez de Arechaga, 'Existencia y caracter juridico del derecho internacional publico' *Revista de derecho internacional* (Junio, 1950) pp. 255–259.

[243] Carneiro, *op. cit.*, p. 97. Also César Díaz Cisneros, 'Fundamento del derecho internacional publico' *Anales de la facultad de ciencias juridicas y sociales de la Universidad de La Plata* (1930) p. 155.

[244] Carneiro, *op. cit.*, pp. 103, 106. Also Velasco Ibarra, *op. cit.*, p. 15. Also Amaro Cavalcanti, 'A renovacao do direito internacional' *Revista de administracao federal, estatal e municipal* (Maio-Junho, 1921) pp. 506–7.

person. Five of these were clearly in favor of including the individual man in this category, but two, though seeming to lean in this direction, were obscure. During the nineteenth century, it will be recalled, none of the systematic publicists entertained such a view. Among the twentieth century "seekers" nearly all those reviewed felt, as did their nineteenth century predecessor, Alberdi, that the individual either does or should enjoy international personality. The only exception was Pedro Baptista Martins, a follower of Kelsen, who was not concerned with this matter.

5. The so-called "new international law" has found many supporters in Latin America. Virtually all of the important schools have been represented, often with interesting variations, together with local views of some significance. It would appear that both among the general treatise writers and among the "seekers," the influence of Duguit has been one of the most notable developments of the twentieth century.

6. While some of the writers of the new international law have grounded their systems on public opinion and solidarity in a positivist-humanist sense, others have employed the conception of solidarity in a naturalistic sense, and one writer was a follower of Kelsen. In all cases the end conclusions have been much the same: (a) the limitation of national sovereignty, (b) recognition of the individual as enjoying international personality (with one exception), and (c) a pronounced emphasis on public opinion or juridical consciousness as either the source or the validator of international law.

CHAPTER IV

AMERICAN INTERNATIONAL LAW

Introduction

A phase of Latin American thought regarding international law which is often mentioned but rarely understood, it seems, is the so-called "American international law."

Although contemporary authors of the highest repute have spoken condescendingly of it [1], there is reason to investigate carefully the ideas concerned, regardless of whether any such analysis may confirm or deny the existence of a characteristically *American* international law. The ideas involved in the alleged school, it is submitted, are some of the fundamental roots of the Pan American system and as such are of the greatest importance to contemporary America [2].

By far the greatest bulk of the literature on this subject has been the contribution of the Chilean jurist, Alejandro O. Alvarez, who, indeed, has been spoken of as a modern Grotius by the Ecuadoran statesman, José María Velasco Ibarra [3]. The sentiments of which Alvarez constantly speaks, however, had existed in Latin America for some time before the Chilean's appearance on the scene; therefore, a number of earlier contributors and their works should be indicated, if for no other reason than to supply the background out of which Alvarez' notions have developed.

The pattern which will be adhered to in this presentation will be as follows: 1. a short historical sketch of some of the

---

[1] Arthur Nussbaum, *A Concise History of the Law of Nations* (New York, The Macmillan Company, 1947), p. 280.

[2] Arthur P. Whitaker, 'Development of American Regionalism' *International Conciliation*, (March, 1951).

[3] José M. Velasco Ibarra, *Experiencias jurídicas hispanoamericanas Bolivar-Alejandro Alvarez-Alberdi* (Buenos Aires, Editorial americalee, 1943), p. 80.

more important aspects of this matter; 2. a survey of the ideas
of Alvarez; 3. a survey of the opposite opinions of Sá Vianna
and Antoko_etz, together with an outline of the views of several
of the more prominent contemporary Latin American scholars
who, in an attempt to determine what the current feeling is
toward the doctrine, have voiced opinions on the matter; and
4. a summary statement.

A. AN HISTORICAL SURVEY

The idea of a characteristically American international law is
of somewhat obscure origin. It is possible that it is in part a
by-product of the circumstances surrounding the independence
movement in Latin America which induced a desire for a greater
break with Europe than eventually transpired.

The Congress of Panama called by Bolivar to meet in 1826,
it will be remembered, was directed toward the end of developing
a political organization for the benefit of the Americas [4]. Although
the pact of "Union, League and Perpetual Confederation" put
forth at the 1826 Congress was never ratified (save by Colombia) [5], the movement itself ultimately resulted in the present
Organization of American States, and in the general hemispheric
cooperation, which includes much of the sentiment embodied
in the whole concept of an American international law.

Certain Latin American foreign offices from time to time have
used the expression, American international law. There was, for
example, the attempt of Mexico in 1834 to call a new American
congress, one of the purposes of which, it was said, would be
to establish foundations of law for governing the mutual relations of the new nations [6]. Similar attempts were made by
the same country in 1838 and in 1840, also to no avail [7]. In
1862 a request of virtually the same sort emanated from the
Peruvian foreign office, which efforts, moreover, culminated in
1866 in a treaty among Bolivia, Chile, Ecuador, and Peru pur-

---

[4] *Ibid.*, p. 51.
[5] Alejandro Alvarez, *Le droit international américain son fondement—sa nature*
(Paris, A. Pedone, 1910), p. 51.
[6] Daniel Antokoletz, *Tratado de derecho internacional público* I (Buenos Aires,
Bernabe y cía, 1944), p. 315.
[7] Alvarez, *loc. cit.*

porting to set forth international law principles; this agreement was signed, but never ratified [8].

At several of the Pan American Conferences attempts were made to promote certain developments of American international law, to which, usually, active opposition arose, as will appear presently [9].

In addition to these official conferences, certain important contributions were made by writers on the subject. According to Díaz Cisneros (1889–   ), the real founder of American international law is Alberdi, and not Alvarez [10], for Díaz Cisneros considers that Alberdi explained this phenomenon in 1844 in a paper presented at the University of Chile for the degree of Licenciado [11]. On the other hand, while in the posthumous works of Alberdi the opinion is expressed that international law in America may be regarded as an American international law in the same sense that domestic law can be English, Roman, or French [12], he also suggests that in actual application the congresses which had been held resulted in no treaties or laws "... which can be called American by [reason of] the extent of their authority [13]." In other words here he seems to feel that American international law is a theoretical possibility which has not materialized.

Furthermore, it has developed that in writings appearing between 1875 and 1891, the Argentine, Vincente G. Quesada (1830–1913), spoke of American international law with reference to such principles as *uti possidetis*. It is of interest to note that Alvarez apparently did not know of this fact until 1924 [14], and, in fact that he once remarked that of the publicists only Alcorta had caught any of the flavor and importance of American international law, but that even he had not understood it at all well [15].

[8] Antokoletz, *op. cit.*, p. 316.

[9] *Ibid.*, pp. 316–317.

[10] César Díaz Cisneros, *Alberdi ante la filosofía y el derecho de gentes* (La Plata, Oliviera y Dominguez, 1930), p. 27.

[11] *Ibid.*, p. 29.

[12] Juan B. Alberdi, 'Politica exterior de la Republica Argentina,' *Escritos póstumos de J. B. Alberdi* Tomo III. (Buenos Aires, Imprenta europea, Moreno y Defensa, 1896), p. 36.

[13] *Ibid.*, p. 37.

[14] César Díaz Cisneros, *Estudios de derecho internacional público* (La Plata, Est. tip. 'Alberdi', M. Sciocco y cía, 1926), pp. 30–31.

[15] Alejandro Alvarez, 'Latin America and International Law' *The American Journal of International Law* (April, 1909), pp. 352–353.

In 1883 a famous polemic took place between Amancio Alcorta and Carlos Calvo in which the former, writing in the *Nueva revista de Buenos Aires*, criticized the latter's work, *Le droit International théorique et pratique* [16], on the grounds that it did not recognize the existence of an American international law. Calvo, in the same journal answered to the effect that he was utterly unable to define this supposed law, that the principles which it allegedly contained were virtually non-existent, and that international law in principle was not subject to distinctions of this sort [17]. Alvarez does not seem to have been aware of this discussion either [18], which, it may be added, was probably the first major debate on this whole problem.

In a later study, previously reviewed, Alcorta takes the only slightly modified position that although he does not pretend that there is in a theoretical sense a characteristically American international law, he does affirm, nevertheless, that in a pragmatic way this law exists [19].

Rodríguez Saráchaga, a close follower of Alcorta [20], took essentially the same position when he observed in 1895 that "... if there is not an essentially American international law, there is nevertheless a series of principles applicable only in America [21]."

The Venezuelan writer, Rafael Fernando Seijas, assumed a somewhat similar position when he wrote in 1884:

The origin of the public and private law of the Hispanic-American republics ought to be looked for in the source of the international differences with foreign powers which have produced inequality in the treatment of the nations of the... hemispheres, obliging us to establish a special [law] which answers to the satisfaction of our aspirations, and to the necessities of our general interests [22].

The question of the existence of an American international law was brought up by Alejandro Alvarez at the Third Latin Ameri-

---

[16] *Supra*, pp. 44–45.

[17] Antokoletz, *op. cit.*, pp. 318–320.

[18] Díaz Cisneros, *Estudios de derecho internacional público*, pp. 29–30.

[19] Amancio Alcorta, *Cours de droit international public* I (Paris, L. Larose et Forcel, 1887) p. 51. See *Supra*, Chapter II.

[20] *Supra*, p. 58.

[21] O. Rodríguez Saráchaga, *El derecho internacional público* (Buenos Aires, Imp. litografia y encuadernacion, 1895), p. 8.

[22] Rafael Fernando Seijas, *El derecho internacional hispano americano* I (Caracas, Imprenta de 'El Monitor,' 1884), p. 511.

can Scientific Congress meeting at Rio de Janeiro in 1905. A resolution to recognize the existence of this particularist law passed the committee but not the congress itself [23].

At the First Pan American Scientific Congress which met in 1908 the question was again brought up and much discussion resulted over the issue of whether a characteristically American international law could be said to exist, or whether it was only that principles of American origin existed as such [24]. This was the second major controversy that arose on this subject [25].

Alvarez was persuaded to modify his resolution with result that the final endorsement by the Congress read as follows:

The First Scientific Pan American Congress recognizes that the difference in the development of the new world compared with that of the old has had the following repercussion on international relations: that in this continent there are problems *sui generis* and also some problems of a clearly American character; [and] that the states of this hemisphere have regulated, by more or less generalized agreements, matters which are of interest only to them or which, being of universal interest, have not yet become susceptible to world wide agreement, by this means incorporating into international law some principles of American origin.

This aggregate of matters constitutes what can be called American problems and situations in international law.

The Scientific Congress recommends to all the states of this continent that in their faculties of jurisprudence and of social sciences, the study of these matters be taken into consideration [26].

Following this conference, Alvarez published in 1910 his famous work, *Le droit international américain,* in which he attempted to show the nature of American international law. In 1912 Sá Vianna published his well known study, *De la non-existence d'un droit international américain* [27], in which is assumed the negative view of the matter. These are the leading works on the problem and will be considered later in more detail.

The third and apparently most recent major round of this

---

[23] Antokoletz, *op. cit.,* p. 320.

[24] *Ibid.,* pp. 320–321. Also Alvarez, *Le droit international américan,* pp. 268–270.

[25] Díaz Cisneros, *Estudios de derecho internacional público,* pp. 31–32.

[26] Alvarez, *Le droit international américain,* pp. 269–270. Also Antokoletz, *op. cit.,* p. 321. The very slight differences between these two quotations in French and Spanish respectively are insignificant.

[27] Manuel Alvaro de Souza Sá Vianna, *De la non-existence d'un droit internationa américain* (Rio de Janeiro, L. Figuredo, 1912).

issue came up in 1923 at the Fifth Pan American Conference at Santiago, Chile [28]. Alvarez held to his original view of the scope of American international law. In this he was opposed by Daniel Antokoletz who felt, as had Sá Vianna in 1908, Alvarez' thesis to be untenable [29].

The quantity of literature from before 1910 almost up to the present has been largely one-sided. Alvarez alone has published a very great deal on this and related topics, while the chief arguments to the contrary consist of those (already mentioned) presented in 1912 by Sá Vianna together with a short section in Antokoletz' treatise on public international law [30].

As has already been noted, the next section of this chapter will survey Alvarez' thesis; this will be followed in turn by the opposite views of Sá Vianna and Antokoletz to which will be added a survey of the views of leading contemporary Latin American writers, together with a short summary of the whole issue.

B. THE THESIS OF ALEJANDRO ALVAREZ

The view of Alejandro Alvarez that a characteristically American international law may be distinguished is, in reality, only a particularistic variation of his theme of solidarity outlined earlier in this work [31].

Alvarez is of the opinion that due to social, psychological, and geographical circumstances, the Americas have consistently entertained a peculiarly intense sentiment of solidarity [32]. This feeling, which he alternately terms sentimentality, mentality, spirit, and psychology, expresses a particular juridical conscience as result of which there have appeared certain features of the governments of the American states that seem to him significantly similar. These may be characterized, he says, as constitutional, republican, democratic, liberal and equalitarian, while seen as being of peaceful intent, as desirous of achieving justice, and by nature idealistic [33].

---

[28] Díaz Cisneros, *Estudios de derecho internacional público*, p. 32.

[29] Antokoletz, *op. cit.*, pp. 321–323.

[30] *Ibid.*, pp. 323–328.

[31] *Supra*, pp. 105–109.

[32] Alvarez, *Le Droit international américain*, pp. 17–21 *et passim*.

[33] Alejandro Alvarez, 'Le developpment du droit des gens dans le nouveau-monde' *Transactions of the Grotius Society* (1940), p. 169.

This outlook, in Alvarez' view, was expressed most cogently by President Monroe in the famed Monroe Doctrine which insisted that European states refrain from intervention in America, and that America no longer be regarded as open to European colonization. He is emphatic that this document expressed American sentiments as a whole, and that it did not represent the mere view of the United States [34]. Jesús María Yepes, follower of Alvarez, goes so far as to say that in taking this position Monroe was strongly influenced by the Colombian envoy to the United States [35].

Alvarez does not, of course, visualize American international law as being antagonistic to international law in general. Rather it is a supplementary element designed to express matters common to America alone [36]. His doctrine is summarized as follows:

By American international law one ought to understand the aggregate of institutions, principles, rules, doctrines, conventions, customs and practices which are characteristic of the American republics in the domain of international relations.

The existence of this law is due to the geographic economic and political conditions of the American continent, to the way in which the new republics were formed and entered into the international community, as well as to the solidarity which exists among them.

American international law understood in this way does not tend in any way to create a system of international law which has for an object the separation of the republics of this hemisphere from the concert of the other nations of the world [37].

One of the alleged virtues of the American international law is, in the opinion of Alvarez, the fusion of the Roman and Anglo-American schools into a Pan American view which, in turn, due to the "liberality of its doctrines," might be expected greatly to influence the future development of international law in

---

[34] Alejandro Alvarez, *International Law and Related Subjects from the Point of View of the American Continent* (Washington, Carnegie Endowment, 1922), p. 37. See also Alvarez, *Le droit international américain*, pp. 137–138 *et passim*. Also Alejandro Alvarez, 'American International Law' *Proceedings of the American Society of International Law*, (1909), p. 209.

[35] J. M. Yepes, *La contribution de l'Amerique Latin au developpment du droit international public et privé* (Paris, Librairie du Recueil Sirey, 1931), pp. 43–45.

[36] Alejandro Alvarez, *Despues de la guerra* (Buenos Aires, Imprenta de la Universidad, 1943), pp. 181–183.

[37] *Ibid.*, pp. 182–183.

general [38]. This position does not imply ultimate universality. On the contrary, one of the cardinal points of Alvarez' view of continentalism is that it is quite consistent with general international law that there should be continental variations [39].

Univeralism, he consistently maintains, is not necessarily a virtue. Well defined principles such as are generally accepted are useful and appropriate, but they should be flexible enough to allow groups of states to develop their intra-group relations in accordance with their particular needs [40]. "There is no attempt", he observes,

to establish two international law orders antagonistic to one another, but only to correct in actual practice the old dogma of absolutism and universality of all rules which make up international law, and to supplement its provisions by a recognition and study of the special problems and conditions which up to this time have been ignored or at best little considered. It is not expected that America shall enjoy special rules as a privilege, but merely that the science of international law shall take into due account and give a just measure of appreciation to the needs of our civilization and to the actualities of our national life [41].

The question is now how to determine with some degree of exactness just what characteristic rules are thought to belong to the American sphere. In this respect Alvarez' works seem disappointing, for at best only a handful of such principles seem to emerge with any degree of concreteness.

In very general terms he mentions some five principal characteristics of American international law. These are: 1. a sentiment of continental solidarity; 2. an American juridical conscience; 3. an American moral conscience; 4. pacificism, idealism, and optimism; and 5. "Respect for law and international morality, condemning all violation of their precepts [42]."

---

[38] Alvarez, *International Law and Related Subjects* ..., p. 22. See also Alejandro Alvarez, *The Monroe Doctrine Its Importance in the International Life of the States of the New World* (New York, Oxford University Press, 1924) p. 31.

[39] Alvarez, *Le droit international américain*, pp. 261–264. Also Alvarez, *Despues de la guerra*, pp. 184–185.

[40] Alvarez, 'American International Law,' p. 216.

[41] *Ibid.*, p. 217.

[42] Alejandro Alvarez, *El continente americano y el nuevo orden social e internacional* (Presentado al consejo directivo del instituto americano de derecho internacional, [c 1940]), p. 21.

These principles are not highly concrete or tangible, but they must be recognized as basic to his general idea, and as affording insight to the basis and nature of the general conception.

Regarding cases, there is not much to be said. Alvarez does mention some concrete examples of rules which, he feels, are essentially American, but many of these can be considered to be obsolete in the sense that there is no longer call for their application; others would seem to have become general in their application regardless of their alleged, and sometimes doubtful, American origin.

Among the rules mentioned are the following: 1. the principle of *uti possidetis* which means, as here applied, that, in 1810 and thereafter when the Latin American states were becoming independent, they established their previous colonial boundaries as national borders [43]; 2. recognition of relatively free and unimpeded fluvial navigation [44]; 3. recognition of the legal status of rebels [45]; 4. recognition of political asylum [46]; 5. acceptance of the principle of *ius soli* as against the generally applied continental principle of *ius sanguinis* [47]; 6. the rule, really a corollary of the first principle here listed, that there is no *res nullius* in America [48]; 7. the equality of states [49]; 8. the Drago Doctrine [50]; and less specifically, 9. the acceptance of codification of international law [51]; and 10. the establishment of arrangements for the defense of this hemisphere [52]. This is in no sense a complete list, but it points up, to some extent, what Alvarez has in mind. A list of American problems, which presumably give rise to uniquely American situations and rules, appears in one of his works [53], but it would not seem to clarify the picture further.

---

[43] Alvarez, *Le droit international américain*, p. 65.

[44] *Ibid.*, pp. 69–70.

[45] *Ibid.*, p. 72.

[46] *Ibid.*, pp. 173–182.

[47] *Ibid.*, pp. 284–290.

[48] Alvarez, 'American International Law', p. 209.

[49] *Loc. cit.*

[50] Alvarez, *Le droit international américain*, pp. 237–240. On this subject see also Luis M. Drago, 'Les emprunts d'état et leurs rapports avec la politique internationale' *Revue generale de droit international public* (1907) pp. 251–287. Also H. A. Moulin, 'La doctrine de Drago' *Revue generale de droit international public* (1907), pp. 417–472.

[51] Alvarez, *Despues de la guerra*, p. 251.

[52] *Loc. cit.*

[53] Alvarez, *Le droit international américain*, pp. 271–277. Regarding specific rules see also Carlos Sánchez i Sánchez, *Curso de derecho internacional publico americano* (Cuidad Trujillo, Editora Montalvo, 1943) pp. 689–896.

All in all, Alvarez is really less concerned with specific rules than with general phenomena such as the sentiment of solidarity of the American states which allegedly induces significantly greater cooperation among these *inter se* than among states chosen at random.

C. OPPOSITION TO THE ALVAREZ THESIS, AND GENERAL LATIN AMERICAN OPINION

1. The Views of Sá Vianna and Antokoletz. Sá Vianna is probably much better known in the United States by virtue of his work denying the existence of an American international law than for his general treatise on international law which has been already noted [54]. The former work was quite obviously prompted by the debate of 1908.

Sá Vianna makes special point of showing that such matters as obligatory arbitration are not exclusively restricted to the new world and not begun there[55]. Moreover, the North Americans and the Latin Americans are observed to be of different temperaments, and the former are inclined to feel themselves superior to the latter in regard to matters of government [56].

Sá Vianna recognizes that ideas such as have originated in America have been incorporated into universal international law, but this he views as merely further evidence against the regional concept and in support of the doctrine of universality [57].

Writing in a philosophical vein he quotes several writers, including Antokoletz, to the effect that the coexistence of American international law and of universal international law is not to be recognized. He implies that only the latter has validity [58], indicating approval, for example, of the view of the Haitian delegate, Leger, to the effect that if the rules of international law express what is just and true, there can be no variation between the hemispheres "... because that which is truth in Europe cannot be error in America, and reciprocally [59]."

---

[54] *Supra*, pp. 91–93.
[55] Sá Vianna, *op. cit.*, pp. 84–180.
[56] *Ibid.*, pp. 53–54.
[57] *Ibid.*, p. 75.
[58] *Ibid.*, pp. 232–233.
[59] *Ibid.*, p. 219.

In view of Sá Vianna's orientation as observed in an earlier place [60], this seems to sum up his objections to the whole idea. While he concedes that the place of the Americas in developing liberal ideas and in working these into the law has been that of a "great admirable and glorious" role, yet he does not feel that the term American international law is appropriately applied thereto [61].

More recently, the negative of the controversy has been taken up by Daniel Antokoletz. This Argentine publicist has attempted to solve the matter with reference to three questions which, in turn, he analyzes.

In the first place, "Can the possibility that an American international law exists be admitted [62]?" By way of answering he notes that conventional regionalism is quite possible and that certain American conventions do, in fact, exist. A clearly constituted system of particularist norms, consequently, is thought to be theoretically possible [63].

Secondly, he asks "Does American international law exist now [64]?" While readily admitting that Pan American solidarity is a reality [65], he has many doubts about the specific applications which have been attributed to it. He is skeptical, for example, about the alleged American origin of so-called fundamental rights of states such as rights of independence and of juridical equality [66]. The notion of arbitration as an American principle draws his criticism: "Neither America nor Europe is anxious to renounce the system of exceptions to arbitration [67]." Codification, he notes, is a European as well as an American phenomenon, and on neither continent is it much beyond infancy [68]. Even *uti possidetis* as a rule of the Americas comes in for a share of criticism as Antokoletz finds that it is not accepted throughout the Americas [69].

---

[60] *Supra*, p. 93.
[61] Sá Vianna, *Loc. cit.*
[62] Antokoletz, *op. cit.*, p. 323.
[63] *Ibid.*, pp. 323–324.
[64] *Ibid.*, p. 324.
[65] *Ibid.*, pp. 324–325.
[66] *Ibid.*, p. 325.
[67] *Ibid.*, p. 326.
[68] *Loc. cit.*
[69] *Ibid.* p. 327.

The following clear and concise statement sums up his answer on this point:

It is affirmed that many principles exist which, by reason of their more or less general acceptance and application, can be considered as constituting the international creed of America. They refer to the sovereign personality of the state, to the proscription of war and of force, to the reign of peace and of law. All that is true and it shows, not the existence of special principles, but of respect and veneration for them [which is] greater in America than in Europe. One may speak of international law *in America*, but not of *American* international law. That does not stop the American nations from drawing up special treaties among themselves more advanced or more humanitarian than [those which govern] their relations with Europe [70].

In the third place, he asks "Is it convenient that there be an international law for the American nations [71]?" To this he replies in substance that: (a) he is generally doubtful; that (b) the American nations (*pueblos*) would prefer to take part in a world wide arrangement as states rather than as subjects of a regional regime which would in some measure supersede them; and that (c) if international law is a science it should be universal [72].

It appears then that both Sá Vianna and Antokoletz recognize an element of truth in the allegations of Alvarez, but that they do not agree with him either as to the scope and extent of the phenomenon in question or in the matter of terminology.

2. *Opinions of a Number of the Better Known Latin American Writers.* A brief survey of a number of the more prominent Latin American writers of international law indicates that prevailing opinion recognizes the existence of problems of international law peculiar to America or of American origin, but that there is little evidence of much strong support for the conception of an American international law in a more extended sense. E. L. Bidau [73], I. Ruiz Moreno [74], L. A. Podestá Costa [75],

---

[70] *Ibid.*, pp. 327–328.

[71] *Ibid.*, p. 328.

[72] *Loc. cit.*

[73] Eduardo L. Bidau, *Derecho internacional publico* I (Buenos Aires, Valerio Abeledo, 1924) p. 11.

[74] Isidoro Ruiz Moreno, *Lecciones de derecho internacional publico* I (Buenos Aires, El ateneo, 1934) p. 64.

[75] L. A. Podestá Costa, *Manual de derecho internacional público* (Buenos Aires, Artes gráficas Bartolomé U. Chiesino, 1947) pp. 24–25.

A. Ulloa [76], M. Cruchaga Tocornal [77], and C. Díaz Cisneros [78] all take, in this respect, much the same view. Even the Santo Domingan, Carlos Sánchez i Sánchez [79] (1895–   ), whose work purports to be a textbook of American public international law, reconciles his discipline with universality. This may be seen in a quotation of his from Alvarez to the effect that American international law is merely an "... *application of the principles of justice* to certain relations of a whole continent [80];" and, again, he makes the observation regarding the term American international law that:

The adjective must not be taken as the expression of a distinct law, but as the expression of a particular application of general and universal public international law [81].

Cruchaga Tocornal, another writer who shows throughout his work much of the influence of Alvarez, notes that the latter never conceived of American international law as opposed to universal international law [82].

As for the others mentioned above, it will suffice here to quote the succinct remark of E. L. Bidau, for it carries the essence also of all of the other views:

If by American international law one must comprehend the existence of exclusively American problems which require peculiar solutions, just as there are European problems which do not interest America, the classification is, in our judgement, acceptable. But this does not authorize us to create a new branch of the science. International law, which develops the juridical constitution of humanity, governs the international community as a whole [83].

Conclusions

The controversy regarding the existence or non-existence of an American international law resolves itself largely into a terminological squabble.

[76] Alberto Ulloa, *Derecho internacional publico* (Lima, Imprenta Torres Aguirre, 1938) pp. 70–75.
[77] Miguel Cruchaga Tocornal, *Derecho internacional* I (Santiago, Chile, Editorial nascimento, 1944), pp. 233–244.
[78] Díaz Cisneros, *Estudios de derecho internacional público*, p. 35.
[79] Sánchez i Sánchez, *op. cit.*, pp. 124–129 *et passim*.
[80] *Ibid.*, p. 127.
[81] *Ibid.*, p. 129.
[82] Cruchaga Tocornal, *op. cit.*, p. 243.
[83] Bidau, *Loc. cit.*

Virtually all of the writers agree that there exists an element of continental solidarity which includes a few peculiarly American rules, practices, and problems, and that America has contributed much to international law in general; but there is much opposition to the term American international law, and to the emphasis on regional pecularities except as being slight variations of general international law. Also, there is much opposition, based often on philosophical grounds, to any suggestion contrary to the idea of universality of international law.

The fact remains that virtually all of the writers who have been concerned with this matter consider that Alvarez' analysis of a sentiment of continental solidarity and community consciousness does have a certain validity. Consequently, on the basis of the adage *ubi societas ibi ius* one could logically contend that the full scope of Alvarez' view is theoretically sound.

On the other hand, if one's theoretical analysis is grounded, for example, on Spiropoulos' view that in all cases the dominant juridical opinion [84] points the way, then it would seem that Alvarez' view is not well founded.

This choice of premises points up much that is of significance in any inquiry into the nature of law. The former, a form of quasi-biological naturalism, assumes a natural result, namely law, flowing from the actual existence of a society. The latter premise, positing a relativist view, suggests that law is essentially an intellectual phenomenon and depends largely not upon the social data *per se*, but upon the social acceptance of a particular juristic view which acceptance may have resulted in no small measure from the persuasive influence of the juristic theory itself. While it is true that the latter normally is based on an evaluation of facts, it is equally true that it is the juridical evaluation and not the facts themselves which dominate the legal horizon. One of this latter persuasion would not admit the active legal significance of a custom which exists in a physical sense but which has been given no juristic consideration. Its existence he would not deny, but he would question its legal reality. Accordingly, one would recognize the potential juridical value of every fact, but would be disposed to require that its

[84] *Supra*, p. 35.

legal significance must be recognized before it can be said to have achieved full juridical reality.

Specifically, one might suggest, for example, that if a government is not recognized (either internally or externally) in spite of the fulfillment of all of the criteria for recognition, who can say that the juridical results normally flowing from recognition would, nevertheless, flow from the fulfillment of the criteria for recognition. Or again, who can deny that shortly after the adoption of the United States Constitution recognition alone accounted for the legal difference between it and the Articles of Confederation? Actually, in view of the fact that the earlier document has never been formally repealed and consequently that it can lay a logical if not a reasonable claim to contemporary validity, one of the main evidences of its invalidity is the mere fact of its not being recognized. Manifestly, sufficient evidence of actual governmental effectiveness may eventually inspire or compel recognition, but in the last analysis only recognition can impute legal significance.

That both of these premises are true to a degree can hardly be denied, but the question of their practical application presents a problem. For example, even assuming the validity of *ubi societas ibi jus*, how does one determine whether a society does or does not exist except by reference to attitudes? Or, what is to prevent opinion from recognizing the existence of a society while denying the application of the adage? And ultimately, what, other than opinion, validates or invalidates the adage itself?

The present writer, holding to a view which combines these premises, is of the opinion that facts, while of potential juridical value, only assume actual legal significance by virtue of recognition of their possession of that legal significance. This recognition is, of course, an intellectual process by which man adjusts his legal rules to conform with his perception of truth. This view does not deny man's ability to perceive truth, nor does it repudiate the validity of natural law in the sense of an intuition of what is just and hence of what ought to be enacted into positive law. Rather, it states that in a human society both truth and justice while having potential juridical value must await appropriate recognition of their attributes before attaining practical legal significance.

In the last analysis, the validity of Alvarez' view must depend on which of the two premises mentioned above appears to be justified together with a judgement as to the extent to which particularist rules actually do obtain. The present writer is of the opinion that there is not sufficient justification for the view advanced by Alvarez. This opinion must be seen, however, in the light of the writer's avowed choice and qualification of premises and from the standpoint of what is believed to be only insignificant variations in continental practices. It must be realized also that there is at least some possibility of future development in the direction of an American international law especially under the auspices of the Organization of American States.

SUMMARY AND CONCLUSIONS

The views on the philosophy of international law of most of the Latin American writers of the nineteenth century, and of selected representative writers of the twentieth century, have been outlined against the background of a general survey of the philosophy of international law since the fifteenth century, and in the light of an explanation of contemporary interest in this general topic. These writers were classified into the three categories of positivist, naturalist, and eclectic, the attempt having been made to give as exact a statement as possible of the position of each on the problem of the nature and sources of international law.

It must be realized, of course, that these three terms have varied in meaning to some degree during the past five hundred years, and that while Grotius was classed as an eclectic by virtue of the views which were generally held in his day, Lauterpacht, who is considered to be a naturalistic thinker, is really much more positivistic than Grotius. There is, then, a certain relativity in these terms which must be recognized by the reader, but at the same time they do suggest similar leanings or tendencies on the part of the writers to whom they are applied which are meaningful so long as the dominant ethos of the age in which the particular writer lived is kept in mind.

In addition to the earlier statements that have been made and by way of refreshing the reader's memory, it would seem appropriate to briefly re-explain the way in which these terms have been used in this work.

The term *positivist* has been applied to those writers who show a marked preference for such sources of international law as treaties, customs, and court decisions, to the relative exclusion of the ideal moral element. *Naturalist*, on the other hand, signifies those writers whose orientation is toward viewing international law as resting primarily on a sense of what is just and

right and only to a small degree on positive sources. Many of
these writers suggest, for example, that the positive law in
order to be valid must mirror the natural law.

The term *eclectic* has been used here in two senses. In the
cases of those writers who are classified as eclectic, it indicates
that the writer being discussed views international law as stemming from treaties and other positive sources on the one hand,
and from a conception of the just on the other. In these instances
the writers seem to give approximately equal weight to naturalist
and to positivist sources and not to rely on one appreciably
more than on the other. The second sense in which the term
eclectic has been used is to be noted in statements observing
that virtually all of the Latin American writers have been,
in fact, eclectics to a degree. This statement means that even
though a writer has stressed treaties and customs and has
belittled the practical importance of natural law, he has not
altogether abandoned it. On the other hand, it describes writers
who have stressed the ideal moral element in the law at the
expense of the positive law, but who, nevertheless, recognize
that the latter does have some significance.

The works of these same writers were analyzed also to determine what stand each would take on the question of the
individual as a subject of international law.

In these phases of the work eighteen writers of each century
were surveyed. In the case of the nineteenth century this figure
represents all of the textbooks and treatises which could be
located. As for the twentieth century the selection was made
in general on the bases of representativeness and importance.

Reform elements were considered separately and the survey
of them does not purport to be exhaustive. Of this group, only
the works of Alberdi were considered in the chapter on the
nineteenth century, while an effort has been made to outline
the more important twentieth century attempts at the reconstruction of the law of nations.

As a whole, the present study attempts to express the general
consensus of textbook and treatise writers in Latin America on
the philosophy of international law; to give a fairly comprehensive estimate of the new view of international law including
proposals and suggestions for reform, as these have appeared

especially in the twentieth century; also to document the increasing support of the view that the individual should be regarded as a subject of international law.

In addition, the question of the existence of an American international law has been surveyed in an attempt to evaluate this particularist theory.

Since nearly all of the Latin American works used in this study have been found available only in Spanish, French, or Portuguese editions, and, for the most part, are not widely known in the United States, it is felt that this survey should contribute to an understanding of Latin American conceptions of international law and to an appreciation of Latin American thought and legal theory in general.

There are essentially six conclusive deductions which may be drawn from this study, and they may be succinctly summarized as follows:

1. Virtually all Latin American publicists reviewed were eclectics to some degree. The classifications of naturalist, eclectic, and positivist are therefore relative designations. These writers show an overwhelming consistency in that all but a very few concern themselves at least to a degree with the ideal moral element as well as with the positive law. This characteristic is in evidence from the earliest to the most modern treatises and stands in marked contrast, for example, to the view presented by Hans Kelsen that the natural law doctrine is at best a useful lie [1].

2. Throughout the entire period covered, the emphasis on positivism has been more pronounced than that on naturalism, but during the twentieth century, positivism has been even more prevalent than during the nineteenth century. This corresponds to the situation elsewhere in the western world. Naturalism, while very much in evidence during this whole period, became less pronounced during the twentieth than it was during the nineteenth century. This is seen in the fact that while there were several works written during the earlier period which

---

[1] Hans Kelsen, 'The Natural Law Doctrine Before the Tribunal of Science' *The Western Political Quarterly*, (December, 1949), p. 513 *et passim*.

could be classified as primarily naturalistic, no such works appeared in the representative twentieth century treatises surveyed. This does not mean that no instances of relatively pure naturalism *exist*; rather, it suggests that this point of view has been tempered with positivism in the minds of writers of systematic treatises, and that naturalism's only appreciable manifestation appears in works sufficiently dichotomous to be classified as eclectic.

3. The attempt made here to document the development of the idea that man as an individual should be entitled to enjoy international personality has indicated rather clearly the increased support in recent time for this important development.

While Alberdi alone among the nineteenth century writers espoused this cause, a considerable number of the more modern scholars have entertained the same view. It is of some significance that approximately a third of the twentieth century writers of general works in Latin America and nearly all of the "seekers" were at least somewhat persuaded in this direction.

It is not known whether this degree of support would obtain throughout the western world as a whole, but the fact that the Latin American ideas on this matter are as strong as they are would lead to the speculation that the status of the individual person in this connection, while manifestly undergoing some change, may be expected in the relatively near future to have become greatly modified.

4. There is ample indication in all of the writings of a fairly close parallel between the philosophy of international law in Latin America and throughout the western world.

As far as the modern influences are concerned, it is evident that the major schools are represented in Latin America together with several uniquely American ideas. It appears that of all the modern reconstructionist schools represented, the view of Duguit has been the most influential.

5. With respect to the sometime controversial question of the existence of a characteristically American international law, it may be concluded that while a few particularistic rules, practices, and sentiments exist as peculiar to the Western Hemisphere, the gist of the polemic seems to be terminological, *i.e.*, the issue seems to be whether this handful of peculiarly American rules

should be called *American* international law, or by the less
formal term of international law *in America*.

There seems to be ample support of Alvarez' view that a
sentiment of continental solidarity does exist in some degree,
but here again the same terminological question is raised as to
whether this sentiment is of enough significance to warrant the
recognition of an American international law.

In the last analysis there seems to be relatively little support
for the American school as such, except as qualified above.

6. As a whole, Latin American views seem to parallel those
of the western world, but there seems to be less adherence in
Latin America to rigid positivism than elsewhere. This is true
in the sense that moral influences, while relegated to lesser
roles more often than not in Hispanic America, are nevertheless
rather consistently recognized as having at least some legal
validity.

In the last analysis two intersting and instructive elements
emerge which are of paramount importance not only for Latin
American jurisprudence but for critical and thoughtful juristic
appraisal everywhere. These are (1) the obviously changing
attitude toward the individual as a subject of the law of nations,
and (2) the feeling of the overwhelming majority of the Latin
American authorities on international law that it is manifestly
unrealistic to try to place juristic naturalism entirely outside
the scope of law.

Of these the former is perhaps the major contemporary issue
of the practical theory of international law. The Latin American
concern with the matter is conterminous with similar attitudes
elsewhere in the world and, as an issue pregnant with potenti-
alities of change, it looms large on the international legal horizon.

The latter is a more purely philosophical consideration and
turns on the question of whether any legal system can avoid
being in some measure eclectic, and in fact, whether the positivists who try either to deny altogether the legal significance of
the moral element or to relegate it entirely to a position anterior
to law have really done anything but confuse the issue by the
use of definitions that delimit too rigidly the broad subject of law.

Latin American eclecticism stands in marked contrast to

relativist views such as Kelsen's belief that the natural law is pure myth and to the Vienna school's proclivity as to the purity of law. It also stands opposed to the Pufendorfian view that only the natural law is valid, but since the last mentioned persuasion has virtually no support today, the importance rests with the Latin American opposition to complete positivism.

That the distinction between law and its moral, sociological, economic, and political formulators is a legitimate and a necessary one should never be allowed to obscure the much more transcendent verity of their intimate connection, and the general Latin American recognition of this fact is a refreshing breath of juristic realism in an atmosphere which has long been too intent upon the exclusiveness of law.

BIBLIOGRAPHY

I. TREATISES, TEXTBOOKS, AND MONOGRAPHS

ACCIOLY, HILDEBRANDO, *Tratado de derecho internacional público*. Rio de Janeiro, Imprensa nacional, 1945–1946. 3 vols.

ALBERDI, JUAN BAUTISTA, *El crimen de la guerra*. [Reprinted from *Escritos póstumos de J. B. Alberdi*]. Buenos Aires, La cultura argentina, 1915. 288 pp.

—— *Escritos póstumos de J. B. Alberdi*, Buenos Aires, Imprenta europea, Moreno y Defensa, 1895–1900. Vols. II, III, and XV.

ALCORTA, AMANCIO, *Cours de droit international public*. I. Paris, L. Larose et Forcel, 1887. 492 pp.

ALVARADO GARAICOA, TEODORO, *Principios normativos del derecho internacional público*. Guayaquil, Imp. de la Universidad, 1946. 395 pp.

ALVAREZ, A., *La codificación del derecho internacional en América*. Santiago de Chile, Imprenta universitaria, 1923. 144 pp.

—— *La codification du droit international ses tendences—ses bases*. Paris, A. Pedone, 1912. 294 pp.

—— *Le continent américain et la codification du droit international une nouvelle "ecole" du droit des gens*. Paris, Les éditions internationales, 1938. 95 pp.

—— *El continente americano y el nuevo orden social e internacional*. (Presentado al consejo directivo del instituto americano de derecho internacional), [c. 1940]. 37 pp.

—— *Despues de la guerra*. Buenos Aires, Imprenta de la Universidad, 1943. 544 pp.

—— *Le droit international américain son fondement—sa nature*. Paris, A. Pedone, 1910. 386 pp.

—— *Le droit international de l'avenir*. Washington, Institut américain de droit international, 1916. 153 pp.

—— *International Law and Relations from the Point of View of the American Continent*. Washington, Carnegie Endowment, 1922. 93 pp.

—— 'Methods for Scientific Codification.' *Science of Legal Method* Vol. IX, pp. 429–497. *The Modern Legal Philosophy Series*, 12 vol. Boston, The Boston Book Company, 1909–17.

—— *The Monroe Doctrine Its Importance in the International Life of the States of the New World*. New York, Oxford University Press, 1924. 573 pp.

—— *Le nouveau droit international public et sa codification en Amérique*. Paris, Librairie Arthur Rousseau, 1924. 66 pp.

—— *La reconstrucción del derecho de gentes. El nuevo orden y la renovacion social*. Santiago, Chile, Editorial nascimento, 1944. 542 pp.

AMERICANO, JORGE, *The New Foundation of International Law*. New York, The Macmillan Company, 1947. 137 pp.

ANTOKOLETZ, DANIEL, *Tratado de derecho internacional público*. Quarta edicion. Buenos Aires, Bernabe y cía, 1944. 3 vols.

ANZILOTTI, DIONISIO, *Cours de droit international*. Paris, Recueil Sirey, 1929. 534 pp.

ARBO, HIGINIO, *Derecho internacional convencional*. Asunción, Imprenta nacional, 1928. 223 pp.

ASPIAZU, AGUSTIN, *Dogmas del derecho internacional*. Nueva York, Imprenta de Hallet and Breen, 1872. 335 pp.

AUSTIN, JOHN, *Lectures on Jurisprudence*. 2 vols. (Edited by R. Campbell), New York, James Crockcroft and Company, 1875.

BÁEZ, CECILIO, *Derecho internacional publico europeo y americano*. Asuncion, Imprenta nacional, 1936. 239 pp.

BELLO, ANDRES, *Obras completas de Don Andres Bello*. Santiago de Chile, Impreso por Pedro G. Ramirez, 1886. Vol. X.

BENTHAM, JEREMY, *The Works of Jeremy Bentham* (published under the superintendence of his executor, John Bowring), XI vols. Edinburgh, William Tait, 1843.

BEVILAQUA, CLOVIS, *Direito publico internacional*. Segunda edição. Rio de Janeiro, Freitas Bastos, 1939. 2 vols.

BIDAU, EDUARDO L., *Derecho internacional publico*. 4a edicion. Buenos Aires, Valerio Abeledo, 1924. 2 vols.

BOURDON-VIANE, G., *Compendio de derecho internacional publico*. Santiago de Chile, Imp. Mejia, 1897. 148 pp.

BRIERLY, JAMES LESLIE, *The Law of Nations* 4th edition. Oxford, The Clarendon Press, 1949. 306 pp.

BUSTAMENTE Y SIRVEN, ANTONIO SANCHEZ DE, *Manual de derecho internacional publico*. Quarta edición. La Habana, La 'Mercantil', 1947. 765 pp.

BYNKERSHOEK, CORNELIUS VAN, *Quaestionum juris publici libri duo*. 1737 edition. In *The Classics of International Law;* translated into English by J. de Louter. Oxford, The Clarendon Press, 1930. 2 vols.

CALVO, CHARLES, *Le droit international théorique et pratique*. Quatrième édition. Paris, Guillaumin et cie., 1887. 5 vols.

CARNEIRO, LEVI, *O direito internavional e a democracia*. Rio de Janeiro, A. Coelho Branco, 1945. 408 pp.

CRAWFORD, WILLIAM REX, *A Century of Latin-American Thought*. Cambridge, Harvard University Press, 1944. 320 pp.

CRUCHAGA TOCORNAL, MIGUEL, *Derecho internacional*. Santiago de Chile, Editorial nascimento, 1944–1948. 2 vols.

DANTAS DE BRITO, A. H., *La philosophie du droit des gens*. Washington, The Catholic University of America Press, 1944. 254 pp.

DÍAZ CISNEROS, CÉSAR, *Alberdi ante la filosofia y el derecho de gentes*. La Plata, Oliviera y Dominquez, 1930. 60 pp.

—— *Estudios de derecho internacional público*. La Plata, Tip. 'Alberdi', M. Sciocco y cía., 1926. 170 pp.

DIEZ DE MEDINA, FEDERICO, *Nociones de derecho internacional moderno*. Paris, Imprenta de Julio Le Clere, 1883. 259 pp.

DUGUIT, LEON, *Law in the Modern State*. New York, B. W. Huebsch, 1919. 247 pp.

EDER, PHANOR J., *A Comparative Survey of Anglo-American and*

Latin American Law. New York, New York University Press, 1950. 257 pp.

ESTEVA RUIZ, D. ROBERTO A., *El derecho publico internacional en Mexico.* Mexico, F. Diaz de Leon, 1911. 84 pp.

FENWICK, CHARLES G., *Cases on International Law.* Chicago, Callaghan and Company, 1935. 815 pp.

—— *International Law.* Third edition. New York, Appleton-Century-Crofts, Inc., 1948. 744 pp.

FERREIRA, D. RAMON, *Lecciones de derecho internacional.* Paraná, Imprenta nacional, 1861. 140 pp.

FIORE, PASQUALE, *International Law Codified and Its Legal Sanction.* New York, Baker, Voorhis and Company, 1918. 750 pp.

FLORES Y FLORES, JOSÉ, *Extracto de derecho internacional.* Guatemala, Tipografia nacional, 1902. 522 pp.

FUENTES, MANUEL A., 'Derecho internacional.' *Curso de enciclopedia del derecho* Tomo III. Lima, Imprenta del estado, 1876. Pp. 1–81.

FULLER, LON L., *The Problems of Jurisprudence.* Brooklyn, The Foundation Press, Inc., 1949. 743 pp.

GARNER, JAMES WILFORD, *Recent Developments in International Law.* Calcutta, The University of Calcutta, 1925. 840 pp.

GENTILI, ALBERICO, *De iure belli libri tres.* 1612 edition. In *The Classics of International Law;* translated into English by J. C. Rolfe. Oxford, The Clarendon Press, 1933. 2 vols.

GROTIUS, HUGO, *De jure belli ac pacis libri tres.* 1646 edition. In *The Classics of International Law;* translated into English by F. W. Kelsey. Oxford, The Clarendon Press, 1925. 2 vols.

HACKWORTH, GREEN HAYWOOD, *Digest of International Law.* Washington, United States Government Printing Office, 1940–44. 8 vols.

HALL, WILLIAM EDWARD, *A Treatise on International Law.* Fourth edition. Oxford, The Clarendon Press, 1895. 791 pp.

—— *A Treatise on International Law.* Seventh edition. Edited by A. Pearce Higgins. Oxford, The Clarendon Press, 1917. 864 pp.

HILL, CHESNEY, *The Doctrine of Rebus Sic Stantibus.* Columbia, The University of Missouri, 1934. 95 pp.

HOBBES, THOMAS, *Philosophical Rudiments Concerning Government and Society* (In *The English Works of Thomas Hobbes* Vol. II edited by William Molesworth). London, John Bohn, 1841. 319 pp.

HOLLAND, THOMAS ERSKINE, *Studies in International Law.* Oxford, The Clarendon Press, 1898. 314 pp.

HYDE, CHARLES CHENEY, *International Law Chiefly as Interpreted and Applied by the United States.* Second edition. Boston, Little, Brown and Company, 1947. 3 vols.

The Inter American System. Washington, Pan American Union, 1947. 32 pp.

JESSUP, PHILIP C., *A Modern Law of Nations.* New York, The Macmillan Company, 1948. 236 pp.

JHERING, RUDOLF VON, *Law as an End in Itself. Modern Legal Philosophy Series.* Vol. V. Boston, The Boston Book Company, 1913. 484 pp.

KALIJARVI, THORSTEN V., *Modern World Politics.* Second edition. New York, Thomas Y. Crowell Company, 1946. 852 pp.

KELSEN, HANS, *General Theory of Law and State*. Cambridge, Harvard University Press, 1945. 516 pp.

—— *Principles of International Law*. New York, Rinehart & Co., 1951. 461 pp.

KENT, JAMES, *Commentaries on American Law*. Twelfth edition. Boston, Little, Brown and Company, 1896. 4 vols.

KRABBE, HUGO, *The Modern Idea of the State*. New York, D. Appleton and Company, 1922. 281 pp.

KUNZ, JOSEF L., *Latin-American Philosophy of Law in the Twentieth Century*. New York, New York University School of Law, 1950. 120 pp.

LAUTERPACHT, HERSH, *The Function of Law in the International Community*. Oxford, The Clarendon Press, 1933. 469 pp.

—— *International Law and Human Rights*. New York, Frederick A. Praeger, Inc., 1950. 475 pp.

LAWRENCE, THOMAS J., *Essays on Some Disputed Questions in Modern International Law*. Cambridge, Deighton Bell and Company, 1885. 313 pp.

—— *Principles of International Law*. Third edition. Boston, Little, Brown and Company, 1900. 681 pp.

LEE, R. W., *Hugo Grotius*. (Proceedings of the British Academy), Vol. XVI. London, Humphrey Milford Amen House, 1930. 63 pp.

LEVI, LEONE, *International Law With Materials for a Code of International Law*. New York, D. Appleton and Company, 1888. 346 pp.

MADIEDO, MANUEL MARÍA, *Tratado de derecho de jentes, internacional, diplomatico i consular*. Bogotá, Tipografia de Nicolas Ponton i compañia, 1874. 549 pp.

MAINE, HENRY SUMNER, *Ancient Law*. Third American—from the fifth London edition. New York, Henry Holt and Company, 1879. 400 pp.

—— *International Law*. New York, Henry Holt and Company, 1888. 234 pp.

MANOTAS WILCHES, EDGARDO, *Le nouveau droit des gens*. Paris, Librairie du Recueil Sirey, 1948. 142 pp.

MARINHO, ILMAR PENNA, *Caracteristicas essencias do novo direito internacional*. Rio de Janeiro, Imprensa nacional, 1947. 475 pp.

MARTINS, PEDRO BAPTISTA, *Da unidade do direito e da supremacia do direito internacional*. 2a edição. Rio de Janeiro, Imprensa nacional, 1942. 90 pp.

MAXEY, CHESTER C., *Political Philosophies*. Revised edition. New York, The Macmillan Company, 1948. 712 pp.

MAZZINI, JOSEPH, 'Duties Toward Your Country.' *Introduction to Contemporary Civilization in the West*. Vol. II. New York, Columbia University Press, 1946. Pp. 344–349.

MERZ, JOHN THEODORE, *Leibniz*. Philadelphia, J. B. Lippincott and Company, 1884. 216 pp.

MILL, JAMES, 'Law of Nations.' *Selected Writings* (of Jeremy Bentham, James Mill, and John Stuart Mill). Garden City, Doubleday Doran and Company, Inc., 1935. Pp. 281–297.

MOORE, JOHN BASSETT, *A Digest of International Law*. Washington, Government Printing Office, 1906. 8 vols.

MORELLI, CIRIACO, *Elementos de derecho natural y de gentes*. [Spanish translation by Dr. Luciano Abeille, Faculty studies of the National University of La Plata, Vol. III, originally published in 1791]. Buenos Aires, Imprenta de Coni Hermanos, 1911. 440 pp.

NUÑEZ ORTEGA, ANGEL (editor). *Derecho internacional mexicano*. Mexico, Imprenta de Gonzalo A. Esteve, 1878, (Partes I y II); Tipografia literaria de Filomeno Mata, 1879, (Parte III). 3 partes (vols.).

NUSSBAUM, ARTHUR, *A Concise History of the Law of Nations*. New York. The Macmillan Company, 1947. 361 pp.

OPPENHEIM, H., *International Law a Treatise*. Second edition. London, Longmans, Green and Company, 1912. 2 vols.

—— *International Law a Treatise*. I. Seventh edition. Edited by H. Lauterpacht. London, Longmans, Green and Company, 1948. 940 pp.

PANDO, JOSÉ MARÍA DE, *Elementos del derecho internacional*. Segunda edicion. Madrid, Imprenta de J. Martin Alegría, 1852. 700 pp.

PEDERNEIRAS, PAUL, *Direito internacional compendiado*. Sexta edição. Rio de Janeiro, A. Coelho Branco, 1938. 430 pp.

PEREZ GOMAR, GREGORIO, *Curso elemental de derecho de gentes*. Montevideo, Imprenta tipográfica a vapor, 1864 (Vol. I); Imprenta de el pueblo, 1866 (Vol. II). 2 vols.

PESSÕA, EPITACIO, *Projecto de codigo de direito internacional publico*. Rio de Janeiro, Imprensa nacional, 1911. 335 pp.

PFANKUCKHEN, LLEWELLYN, *A Documentary Textbook in International Law*. New York, Farrar and Rinehart, Inc., 1940. 1030 pp.

PHILLIMORE, ROBERT JOSEPH, *Commentaries Upon International Law*. I. Philadelphia, T. and J. W. Johnson, Law Booksellers, 1854. 394 pp.

PLANAS SUÁREZ, D. SIMÓN, *Tratado de direcho internacional público*. Madrid, Hijos de Reus, 1916. 2 vols.

PODESTÁ COSTA, L. A., *Manual de derecho internacional público*. Segunda edición. Buenos Aires, Artes gráficas Bartolomé U. Chiesino, 1947. 536 pp.

POLITIS, NICOLAS, *The New Aspects of International Law*. Washington, Carnegie Endowment for International Peace, 1928. 86 pp.

POTTER, PITMAN B., *A Manual Digest of Common International Law*. New York, Harper and Brothers, 1932. 284 pp.

PUFENDORF, SAMUEL VON, *Of the Law of Nature and Nations*. Third edition. Translated by Basil Kennet. London, Sare, Bonwicke, Goodwyn, Walthoe, Wotton, *et al.*, 1717. 212+577+531 pp.

—— *De officio hominis et civis juxta legem naturalem libri duo*. 1682 edition. In *The Classics of International Law;* translated into English by P. G. Moore. New York, Oxford University Press, 1927. 2 vols.

RACHEL, SAMUEL, *De jure naturae et gentium dissertationes*. 1676 edition. In *The Classics of International Law;* translated into English by J. P. Bate. Baltimore, The Lord Baltimore Press, 1916. 2 vols.

RAMIREZ, JOSÉ H., *Codigo de los extranjeros; introducción al estudio del derecho internacional desde los tiempos antiguos hasta nuestros dias*. Mexico, Imprenta de I. Escalante y ca., 1870. 244 pp.

RAMÓN RIBEYRO, D., *Derecho internacional público*. Lima, Libreria escolar é imprenta de E. Moreno, 1901–5. 2 vols.

RECASÉNS SICHES, LUIS; COSIO, CARLOS; LLAMABÍAS DE AZEVEDO, JUAN; GARCÍA MÁYNEZ, EDUARDO, *Latin-American Legal Philosophy*. (20th Century Legal Philosophy Series, Vol. III). Cambridge, Harvard University Press, 1948. 557 pp.

RODRIGUES PEREIRA, LAFAYETTE, *Principios de direito internacional*. Rio de Janeiro, Jacintho Ribeiro dos Santos, 1902–3. 2 vols.

RODRIGUEZ CERNA, JOSE, *Nuestro derecho internacional. Sinopsis de tratados y anotaciones historicos 1921–37*. Guatemala, 1938. 816 pp.

RODRÍGUEZ SARÁCHAGA, O., *El derecho internacional público*. Buenos Aires, Imp. litografía y encuadernación, 1895. 692 pp.

RUIZ MORENO, ISIDORO, *Lecciones de derecho internacional publico*. Buenos Aires, El ateneo, 1934–5. 3 vols.

RUIZ MORENO, ISIDORO (h.), *El pensamiento internacional de Alberdi*. Buenos Aires, Imprenta de la Universidad, 1945. 137 pp.

SAÉNZ, ANTONIO, *Instituciones elementales sobre el derecho natural y de gentes*. [Curso dictado en la Universidad de Buenos Aires en los años 1822–3]. (This is Vol. I of a series entitled *Coleccion de textos y documentos para la historia del derecho argentina*, put out by the Facultad de derecho y ciencias sociales, instituto de historia del derecho argentina). Buenos Aires, A. Baiocca y cía., 1939. 357 pp.

SALAZAR, D. RAMON Y FEDERICO S. DE TEJADA, *Derecho internacional guatemalteco*. Guatemala, Tipografia y encuadernacion (Tomo I); Tipografia nacional (Tomas II y III), 1892–1919. 3 vols.

SÁNCHEZ I SÁNCHEZ, CARLOS, *Curso de derecho internacional publico americano*. Cuidad Trujillo, Editora Montalvo, 1943. 729 pp.

SÁ VIANNA, MANOEL ALVARADO DE SOUZA, *Elementos de direito internacional*. I. Rio de Janeiro, Tip. do jornal do commercio, de Rodrigues & c., 1908. 318 pp.

—— *De la non-existence d'un droit international américain*. Rio de Janeiro, L. Figueredo-editeur, 1912. 290 pp.

SCHLESINGER RUDOLF, *Soviet Legal Theory*. London, Kegan Paul, Trench, Trubner & Co., Ltd., 1946. 299 pp.

SCOTT, JAMES BROWN, *The Catholic Conception of International Law*. Washington, Georgetown University Press, 1934. 494 pp.

—— *The Spanish Origin of International Law*. Oxford, The Clarendon Press, 1934. 288 pp.

SEIJAS, RAFAEL FERNANDO, *El derecho internacional hispano americano*. Caracas, Imprenta de 'El Monitor,' 1884. 6 vols.

SERENI, ANGELO PIERO, *The Italian conception of International Law* (New York, Columbia University Press, 1943. 402 pp.

SILVA SANTISTEBAN, JOSÉ, *Curso de derecho internacional*. Segunda edicion. Lima, A. Aubert y comp., 1864. 214 pp.

SPINOZA, BENEDICT, *The Chief Works of Benedict de Spinoza*. (Translated from the Latin with an introduction by R. H. M. Elwes). London, George Bell and Sons, 1883. 2 vols.

SPIROPOULOS JEAN, *Théorie générale du droit international*. Paris, Librairie générale de droit & de jurisprudence, 1930. 220 pp.

TARACOUZIO, T. A., *The Soviet Union and International Law*. New York, The Macmillan Company, 1935. 530 pp.

TEXTOR, JOHANN WOLFGANG, *Synopsis juris gentium*. 1680 edition. In *The Classics of International Law;* translated into English by J. P. Bate. Washington, The Carnegie Institution, 1916. 2 vols.

Torre, Juan de la, *Guia para el estudio del derecho constitucional mexicano*. Mexico, Tip. de J. V. Villada, 1886. 392 pp.

Treitschke, Heinrich von, 'Politics.' *Introduction to Contemporary Civilization in the West*. Vol. II. New York, Columbia University Press, 1946. Pp. 763–779.

Tremosa y Nadal, Angel, *Nociones de derecho internacional*. Habana, 'La Australia,' 1896. 221 pp.

Triepel, Heinrich, *Droit international et droit interne*. Paris, A. Pédone, 1920. 448 pp.

Ulloa, Alberto, *Derecho internacional público*. I. Segunda edición. Lima, Imprenta Torres Aguirre, 1938. 394 pp.

Ursúa, Francisco A, *Derecho internacional publico*. Mexico, Editorial 'Cultura', 1938. 477 pp.

Vasconcellos Menzes de Drummond, Antonio de, *Prelecções de direito internacional*. Pernambuco, Tipographia do correio do Recife, 1867. 233 pp.

Vattel, Emir de, *Le droit de gens, ou principes de la loi naturelle, appliqués à la conduite et aux affaires des nations et des souverains*. 1758 edition. In *The Classics of International Law;* translated into English by C. G. Fenwick. Washington, The Carnegie Institution, 1916. 3 vols.

Velasco Ibarra, José M., *Derecho internacional del futuro*. Buenos Aires, Editorial Americalee, 1943. 209 pp.

—— *Experiencias juridicas hispanoamericanas Bolivar-Alejandro Alvarez-Alberdi*. Buenos Aires, Editorial Americalee, 1943. 154 pp.

Victoria, Francisci de, *De indis et de iure belli relectiones*. 1696 edition. In *The Classics of International Law;* translated into English by J. P. Bate. Washington, The Carnegie Institution, 1917. 475 pp.

Vreeland, Hamilton, *Hugo Grotius*. New York, Oxford University Press, 1917. 258 pp.

Walker, Thomas A., *A History of the Law of Nations*. I. Cambridge, Cambridge University Press, 1899. 361 pp.

Wharton, Frances, *A Digest of the International Law of the United States*. Washington, Government Printing Office, 1886. 3 vols.

Wheaton, Henry, *Elements of International Law*. Second annotated edition by W. B. Lawrence. Boston, Little Brown and Company, 1863. 1095 pp.

Wilson, George Grafton, *International Law*. New York, Silver, Burdett and Company, 1935. 372 pp.

Yepes, Jesús María, *Alejandro Alvarez créateur du droit international américain*. Paris, Les éditions internationales, 1938. 31 pp.

—— *La contribution de l'Amérique Latin au développement du droit international public et privé*. Paris, Recueil Sirey, 1931. 109 pp.

—— *El panamericanismo y el derecho internacional*. Bogotá, Imprenta nacional, 1930. 447 pp.

Zeballos, Don Estonislao S., *International Law of Spanish America. Arbitration on Misiones*. Buenos Aires, Jacobo Peuser, 1893. 111 pp.

Zouche, Richard, *Juris et judicii feciales, sive juris inter gentes, et quaestionum de eodem explicatio*. 1650 edition. In *The Classics of International Law;* translated into English by J. L. Brierly. Baltimore, The Lord Baltimore Press, 1911. 2 vols.

II. ARTICLES

ALVAREZ, A., 'American International Law.' (*Proceedings of the American Society of International Law*. Third annual meeting. Pp. 206–219. 1909).
—— 'La conférence des juristes de Rio de Janeiro et la codification du droit international américain.' (*Revue générale de droit international public*. Tome XX. Pp. 24–52. 1913).
—— 'Le développement du droit des gens dans le nouveau-monde.' (*Transactions of The Grotius Society*. Vol. 25. Pp. 169–184. 1940).
—— 'Le droit international américain. Son origine et son évolution.' (*Revue générale de droit international public*. Tome XIV. Pp. 393–405. 1907).
—— 'La futura sociedad de las naciones.' (*Actas memorias y proyectos de las sesiones de La Habana; Instituto americano de derecho internacional*. Segunda reunion. Pp. 242–305. 1918).
—— 'Latin America and International Law.' (*The American Journal of International Law*. Vol. 3. Pp. 269–353. April, 1909).
—— 'De la necesidad de una nueva concepción del derecho.' (*Anales de la Universidad*. Republica de Chile. Tomo CXLVI. Pp. 175–198. 1920).
—— 'The Necessity for the Reconstruction of International Law—Its Aim.' (*Proceedings of the Fourth Conference of Teachers of International Law and Related Subjects*. Pp. 11–16. 1930).
—— 'New Conception and New Bases of Legal Philosophy.' (*Illinois Law Review*. Vol. XIII. Pp. 167–182. 1918–9).
—— 'The New International Law.' (*Transactions of the Grotius Society*. Vol.15. Pp. 35–48. 1930).
—— 'Le nouveau droit des gens et le projet d'une école internationale de droit international.' (*Revue de droit international et de législation comparée*. Troisième série, Tome I. Pp. 149–158. 1920).
—— 'Les sources du droit des gens.' (*Annuaire de l'institut de droit international*. Session de Paris. Pp. 490–507. Octobre, 1934).
ALVAREZ PRADO, J. R., 'Teoria del derecho internacional.' (*Revista de ciencias jurídicas y sociales*. Año XII. Pp. 211–216. 1947).
CAVALCANTI, AMARO, 'A renovação do direito internacional.' (*Revista de direito publico e de administração federal, estatal e municipal*. Vol. I. Pp. 503–528. 1921).
CHAKSTE, MINTAUTS, 'Soviet Concepts of the State, International Law and Sovereignty.' (*The American Journal of International Law*. Vol. 43. Pp. 21–36. January, 1949).
DÍAZ CISNEROS, CÉSAR, 'Fundamento del derecho internacional publico.' (*Anales de la facultad de ciencias jurídicas y sociales de la Universidad de La Plata*. Tomo V. Pp. 145–165. 1930).
DICKINSON, EDWIN D., 'Changing Concepts and the Doctrine of Incorporation.' (*The American Journal of International Law*. Vol. 26. Pp. 239–260. April, 1932).
DRAGO, LUIS M., 'Les emprunts d'état et leurs rapports avec la politique internationale.' (*Revue générale de droit international public*. Pp. 251–287. 1907).

DUGUIT, LEON, 'Objective Law' (Translated by Margaret Grandgent). (*Columbia Law Review*. Vol. 20, pp. 817–831; vol. 21, pp. 17–34, 126–143, 242–256. 1920, 1921).

FLORIN, JOSEPH AND JOHN H. HERZ, 'Bolshevist and National Socialist Doctrines of International Law.' (*Social Research*. Vol. 7. Pp. 1–31. February, 1940).

HAZARD, JOHN N., 'Cleansing Soviet International Law of Anti-Marxist Theories.' (*The American Journal of International Law*. Vol. 32. Pp. 244–252. April, 1938).

HERZ, JOHN H., 'The National Socialist Doctrine of International Law and the Problems of International Organization.' (*Political Science Quarterly*. Vol. LIV. Pp. 536–554. December, 1939).

HUMPHRY, JOHN P., 'On the Foundations of International Law.' (*The American Journal of International Law*. Vol. 39. Pp. 231–243. April, 1945).

JACOBINI, H. B., 'Some Observations Concerning Jeremy Bentham's Concepts of International Law.' (*The American Journal of International Law*. Vol. 42. Pp. 415–417. April, 1948).

JIMENEZ DE ARECHAGA, EDUARDO, 'Existencia y caracter juridico del derecho internacional publico.' (*Revista de derecho internacional*. Tomo LVII. Pp. 198–269. Junio, 1950).

KELSEN, HANS, 'The Natural Law Doctrine Before the Tribunal of Science.' (*The Western Political Quarterly*. Vol. II. Pp. 481–513. December, 1949).

KORFF, S. A., 'An Introduction to the History of International Law'. (*The American Journal of International Law*. Vol. 18. Pp. 246–259. April, 1924).

KOROVIN, EUGENE A., 'The Second World War and International Law.' (*The American Journal of International Law*. Vol. 40. Pp. 742–755. October, 1946).

KULSKI, W. W., 'Soviet Comments on International Law' (*American Journal of International Law*. Vols. 45, 46, 47. 1951, 1952, 1953).

KUNZ, JOSEF L., 'The Meaning and the Range of the Norm *Pacta Sunt Servanda*.' (*The American Journal of International Law*. Vol. 39. Pp. 180–197. April, 1945).

LAUTERPACHT, H., 'The So-Called Anglo-American and Continental Schools of Thought in International Law.' (*The British Year Book of International Law*. Vol. 12. Pp. 31–62. 1931).

—— 'Spinoza and International Law.' (*The British Year Book of International Law*. Vol. 8. Pp. 89–107. 1927).

MONTMORENCY, J. E. G. DE, 'Thomas Hobbes.' (*Journal of Comparative Legislation*. Vol. 8. Pp. 51–70. 1907).

MOULIN, H. A., 'La doctrine de Drago.' (*Revue générale de droit international public*. Pp. 417–472. 1907).

OPPENHEIM, L., 'The Science of International Law: Its Task and Method.' (*The American Journal of International Law*. Vol. 2. Pp. 313–356. April, 1908).

PHILLIPSON, COLEMAN, 'Samuel Pufendorf.' (*Journal of Comparative Legislation*. Vol. 12. Pp. 233–265. 1911).

REVES, JESSE S., 'The Influence of the Law of Nature Upon International Law in the United States.' (*The American Journal of International Law*. Vol. 3. Pp. 547–561. July, 1909).

Sandelius, Walter E., 'The Question of Sovereignty and Recent Trends of Juristic Thought.' *Twentieth Century Political Thought.* (Edited by J. S. Roucek). New York, Philosophical Library, 1946. Pp. 149–170.

Scott, James Brown, 'The Modern Law of Nations and Its Municipal Sanctions.' (*The Georgetown Law Journal.* Vol. XXII. Pp. 131–206. January, 1934).

—— 'Francisco Suarez His philosophy of Law and of Sanctions.' (The Georgetown-Law Journal, 1934).

Starke, J. G., 'Monism and Dualism in the Theory of International Law.' (*The British Year Book of International Law.* Vol. 17. Pp. 66–81. 1936).

Verdross, Alfred von, 'On the Concept of International Law.' (*The American Journal of International Law.* Vol. 43. Pp. 435–440. July, 1949).

Whitaker, Arthur P., 'Development of American Regionalism.' (*International Conciliation.* No. 469. Pp. 123–164. March, 1951).

Willoughby, W. W., 'The Legal Nature of International Law.' (*The American Journal of International Law.* Vol. 2. Pp. 357–365. April, 1908).

Wright, Quincy, 'International Law in its Relation to Constitutional Law.' (*The American Journal of International Law.* Vol. 17. Pp. 234–244. April, 1923).

III. BIBLIOGRAPHICAL LITERATURE

Backus, Richard C. and Phanor J. Eder, *A Guide to the Law and Legal Literature of Columbia.* Washington, The Library of Congress, 1943. 222 pp.

Bishop, Crawford M. and Anyda Marchant, *A Guide to the Law and Legal Literature of Cuba the Dominican Republic and Haiti.* Washington, The Library of Congress, 1944. 276 pp.

Borchard, Edwin M., *Guide to the Law and Legal Literature of Argentina, Brazil and Chile.* Washington, Government Printing Office, 1917. 523 pp.

Clagett, Helen L., *A Guide to the Law and Legal Literature of Argentina 1917–46.* Washington, The Library of Congress, 1948. 180 pp.

—— *A Guide to the Law and Legal Literature of Bolivia.* Washington, The Library of Congress, 1947. 110 pp.

—— *A Guide to the Law and Legal Literature of Chile 1917–46.* Washington, The Library of Congress, 1947. 103 pp.

—— *A Guide to the Law and Legal Literature of Ecuador.* Washington, The Library of Congress, 1947. 100 pp.

—— *A Guide to the Law and Legal Literature of Paraguay.* Washington, The Library of Congress, 1947. 59 pp.

—— *A Guide to the Law and Legal Literature of Peru.* Washington, The Library of Congress, 1947. 188 pp.

—— *A Guide to the Law and Legal Literature of Uruguay.* Washington, The Library of Congress, 1947. 123 pp.

—— *A Guide to the Law and Legal Literature of Venezuela.* Washington, The Library of Congress, 1947. 128 pp.

VANCE, JOHN T. AND HELEN L. CLAGETT, *A Guide to the Law and Legal Literature of Mexico*. Washington, The Library of Congress, 1945. 269 pp.

IV. ENCYCLOPAEDIA ARTICLES

BERNARD, L. L., 'Alberdi, Juan Bautista.' *The Encyclopaedia of the Social Sciences* Vol. 1. New York, The Macmillan Company, 1937. P. 613.

BONNARD, ROGER, 'Duguit, Leon.' *The Encyclopaedia of the Social Sciences* Vol. 5. New York, The Macmillan Company, 1932. Pp. 69–72.

COTTIN, GEORGE E., 'Hobbes, Thomas.' *The Encyclopaedia of the Social Sciences* Vol. 7. New York, The Macmillan Company, 1932. Pp. 394–396.

GURVITCH, GEORGE, 'Natural Law.' *The Encyclopaedia of the Social Sciences* Vol. 11. New York, The Macmillan Company, 1932. Pp. 284–290.

LEVI, ALESANDRO, 'Mancini, Pasquele Staneslao.' *The Encyclopaedia of the Social Sciences* Vol. 10. New York, The Macmillan Company, 1932. P. 84.

V. DOCUMENTS

Charter of the United Nations Together with the Statute of the International Court of Justice. [Washington], U. S. Government Printing Office, 1945. 58 pp.

International Civil Aviation Conference. [Department of State Publication 2282 Conference Series 64]. Washington, U. S. Government Printing Office, 1945. 284 pp.

'International Military Tribunal (Nuremberg), Judgment and Sentences.' (*The American Journal of International Law*. Vol. 41. Pp. 172–333. January, 1947).

The Proceedings of the Hague Peace Conferences. (Translation of the official texts). 1 volume of the Conference of 1899, 3 volumes of the Conference of 1907, and an index volume. New York, Oxford University Press, 1920–1.

VI. WORKS CITED BUT NOT SEEN BY THE WRITER

These titles were cited in the text or footnotes as referring to works which could not be, or were thought unnecessary that they should be, checked by the present writer, or, in the interest of completeness, as works pertinent to Chapter II but which could not be located for use.

ACOSTA Y LARA, FEDERICO, *Apuntes para un curso de derecho internacional publico*. Uruguay, 1896.

ALÇANDARA, BELLAGARDE, *Noçoes elementos de direito dos gentes*. Brazil, 1851.

AZCÁRATE, *El derecho internacional americano*. 1898.

BARROS, JOSÉ MARIA, *Elementos de derecho internacional por Henry Wheaton*. Mexico, Impr. de J. M. Lara, 1854–5. 2 vols.

BLUNTSCHLI, JOHANN KASPAR, *Das moderne Völkerrecht der civilisirten Staaten als Rechtsbuch dargestellt*. Nördlingen, C. H. Beck, 1878. 541 pp.

FIELD, DAVID DUDLEY, *Draft Outlines of an International Code*. New York, Diossy and Company, 1872. 2 vols.

FIORE, PASQUALE, *Trattato di diritto internazionale pubblico*. Torino, Unione tipografico, 1887–91. 3 vols.

GAENAGA, MAGNASCO, Y ECHAIDA, *Notas sobre el derecho internacional publico y privado*. Argentina, 1883.

HEFFTER, AUGUST WILHELM, *Das europäische Völkerrecht der Gegenwart auf den bisherigen Grundlagen*. Berlin, E. H. Schraeder, 1844. 412 pp.

JELLINEK, GEORG, *Der Rechtliche Natur der Staatenverträge*. Wien, A. Holder, 1880. 66 pp.

KAUFMANN, ERICH, *Das Wesen des Völkerrechts und die clausula rebus sic stantibus*. Tübingen, J. C. B. Mohr, 1911. 231 pp.

KLÜBER, JOHANN LUDWIG, *Droit des gens moderne de l'Europe*. Stuttgart, J. G. Cotta, 1819. 2 vols.

LE FUR, LOUIS E., *Précis de droit international public*. Deuxième édition. Paris, Librairie Dalloz, 1933. 603 pp.

LEGUIZAMÓN, ONÉSIMO, *Apuntes sobre el programa oficial del primer curso*, tomados por Luis T. Pintos y Joaquín Rivadavia. Argentina, 1874.

LUNA, ANTONIO, *Manual del estudiante sobre derecho internacional*. Argentina, 1884.

MANCINI, PASQUALE STANESLAO, *Diritto internazionale*. Roma, Unione tip. Manuzio, 1905. 202 pp.

MARTENS, GEORG FRIEDRICH VON, *Précis du droit des gens moderne de l'Europe*. Deuxième édition. Gottingue, Dieterich, 1801. 502 pp.

MARTINEZ SILVA, CARLOS, *Notas a la obra de Bello*. Colombia, 1883.

MATTA, PEDRO DA AUTRAM E ALBUQUERQUE, *Elementos de direito das gentes*. Brazil, 1851.

MONTEFAR, LORENZO, *Nociones de derecho de gentes y leyes de la guerra*. Guatemala, 1893.

MOSER, JOHANN JAKOB, *Versuch des neuesten europäischen Völkerrechts in Friedens—und Kriegszeiten, vernehmlich aus denen Staatshandlungen derer europäischen Mächten, auch anderen Begebenheiten, so sich seit dem Tode Kaiser Karls VI in Jahre 1740 zugetragen haben*. Frankfurt am Mayn, Varrentrapp sohn und Wenner, 1777–80. 10 vols.

PEREIRA, PINTO, *Apuntomentos para o direito internacional*. Brazil, 1864.

PINTO, LUIS T., JOAQUÍN RIVADAVIA, Y ONÉSIMO LEGUIZAMÓN, *Derecho internacional*. Argentina, 1894. (This title and that of Leguizamón listed above may refer to the same work).

PRADIER-FODÉRÉ, PAUL L. E., *Traité de droit international public européen et américain*. Paris, G. Pedone-Lauriel, 1885–1906. 8 vols.

SAVIGNY, FRIEDRICH K. VON, *Of the Vocation of Our Age for Legislation and Jurisprudence*. London, Littlewood and Company, 1831. 192 pp.

SUAREZ, *Compendio de derecho internacional de don Andrés Bello*. Chile, 1883.

WOLFF, CHRISTIAN VON, *Jus gentium methodo scientifica pertractatum*. 1764 edition. In *The Classics of International Law;* translated into English by J. H. Drake. Oxford, The Clarendon Press, 1934. 2 vols.

INDEX

Garner, J. W. 31
Gentile, A. 13–14
German naturalism 21–23
Grotian school 26
Grotianism, twentieth century positivistic 30
Grotius, H. 12, 14–15

H

Hackworth, G. H. 29
Hague Conventions 29
Hall, W. E. 29
Heffter, A. W. 27
Hegel, G. W. H. 17
Historical school 26
History of international law (see international law)
Hobbes, T. 16–17

I

Incorporation, doctrine of 31–33
International law, history of 12–37
Italian school 21, 24

J

Jellinek, G. 23
Jessup, P. 36
Jhering, R. von 23

K

Kaufmann, E. 23
Kelsen, H. 3, 33–34
Kelsen, views of compared with those of Lauterpacht 2–4
Kelsen, influence of in Latin America 104, 112-113, 120, 111-112
Kent, J. 28
Klüber, J. L. 27
Korovin, Y. A. 25
Krabbe, H. 33

L

Latin American theories of international law, relation of to western political thought in general 37, 76, 120, 139, 140
Lauterpacht, H. 4, 28, 35–36
Lauterpacht, views of compared with those of Kelsen 2–4

Lawrence, T. J. 28
Le Fur, L. E. 2, 28, 34
Le Fur, influence of in Latin America 101, 102, 103, 109–111
Leguizamón, O. 74
Leibnitz, G. W. 19
Levi, L. 28
Luna, A. 74

M

Madiedo, M. M. 51–53
Magnasco 74
Maine, H. J. S. 26
Man as a subject of international law 35–36, 70–72, 75, 81–82, 85, 87–88, 92–93, 97–98, 100, 101, 102, 108–109, 111, 113, 116, 118–119, 119–120, 140, 141
Mancini, P. S. 24
Manotas Wilches, E. 109–111
Marinho, I. P. 117–119
Martens, G. F. von 15–16
Martinez, S. C. 74
Martins, P. B. 111–113
Matta, P. da A. e Albuquerque 50, 74
Mazzini, G. 24
Mill, James 17–18, 26
Monist theories 33–34
Montefar, L. 74
Moore, J. B. 29
Morelli, C. 73
Mortensen v. Peters, case of 32
Moser, J. J. 15

N

Natural law compared with positive law 2
Naturalism in the history of international law 12–37, especially 12–13, 16–17, 18–20, 28
Naturalists, nineteenth century Latin American 58–67
Naturalism, influence of in Latin America 74–75, 119–120, 139–140, 141–142
New international law 8–9, 33–37, 72, 75, 104–119, 120, 138-139, 140
Nuñez Ortega, A. 72
Nuremberg Trials 36